Grand River Collegiate Institute

Figure Skating

Other titles in the Science Behind Sports series:

Figure Skating

JENNY MACKAY

LUCENT BOOKS

A part of Gale, Cengage Learning

GALE
CENGAGE Learning·

Detroit • New York • San Francisco • New Haven, Conn • Waterville, Maine • London

LIBRARY OF CONGRESS CATALOGING-IN-PUBLICATION DATA

MacKay, Jenny, 1978-
  Figure skating / by Jenny MacKay.
    p. cm. -- (The science behind sports)
  Includes bibliographical references and index.
  ISBN 978-1-4205-0784-3 (hardcover)
 1. Figure skating--Juvenile literature. 2. Sports sciences--Juvenile literature. I. Title.
  GV850.4.M32 2012
  796.91'2--dc23

                                                        2012002239

Lucent Books
27500 Drake Rd
Farmington Hills MI 48331

ISBN-13: 978-1-4205-0784-3
ISBN-10: 1-4205-0784-2

Printed in the United States of America

1 2 3 4 5 6 7 16 15 14 13 12

TABLE OF CONTENTS

FOREWORD

On March 21, 1970, Slovenian ski jumper Vinko Bogataj took a terrible fall while competing at the Ski-flying World Championships in Oberstdorf, West Germany. Bogataj's pinwheeling crash was caught on tape by an ABC *Wide World of Sports* film crew and eventually became synonymous with "the agony of defeat" in competitive sporting. While many viewers were transfixed by the severity of Bogataj's accident, most were not aware of the biomechanical and environmental elements behind the skier's fall—heavy snow and wind conditions that made the ramp too fast and Bogataj's inability to maintain his center of gravity and slow himself down. Bogataj's accident illustrates that, no matter how mentally and physically prepared an athlete may be, scientific principles—such as momentum, gravity, friction, and aerodynamics—always have an impact on performance.

Lucent Book's Science Behind Sports series explores these and many more scientific principles behind some of the most popular team and individual sports, including baseball, hockey, gymnastics, wrestling, swimming, and skiing. Each volume in the series focuses on one sport or group of related sports. The volumes open with a brief look at the featured sport's origins, history and changes, then move on to cover the biomechanics and physiology of playing, related health and medical concerns, and the causes and treatment of sports-related injuries.

In addition to learning about the arc behind a curve ball, the impact of centripetal force on a figure skater, or how water buoyancy helps swimmers, Science Behind Sports readers will also learn how exercise, training, warming up, and diet and nutrition directly relate to peak performance and enjoyment of the sport. Volumes may also cover why certain sports are popular, how sports function in the business world, and which hot sporting issues—sports doping and cheating, for example—are in the news.

Basic physical science concepts, such as acceleration, kinetics, torque, and velocity, are explained in an engaging and accessible manner. The full-color text is augmented by fact boxes, sidebars, photos, and detailed diagrams, charts and graphs. In addition, a subject-specific glossary, bibliography and index provide further tools for researching the sports and concepts discussed throughout Science Behind Sports.

CHAPTER 1

A History of Figure Skating

Figure skating is one of the most popular winter spectator sports in the world. Every four years during the Winter Olympics, more people watch the figure skating competitions than any other televised portion of the Games. Elegant costumes and mesmerizing skating routines set to music make modern figure skating an artistic performance as much as a sport. As entertaining as it may be to watch, carrying out a skating routine on ice is an incredibly complex and difficult athletic endeavor that requires skaters to be in peak physical condition and spend countless hours practicing their craft. Professional skaters always strive to bring something new and fresh to their performances, impressing audiences with stunts that have never been done before. This is no small feat, considering humans have been propelling themselves across ice on skates for about four thousand years. Figure skaters build constantly on a long history of methods and techniques in their quest to master a sport that demands as much creativity and grace as strength and precision.

Early Ice-Skating

Skating may be among the oldest of human pastimes, but it has not always been a globally popular one. Places close to the equator tend to have a hot climate all year long, and

people who live in these places rarely, if ever, see snow or ice. The farther a person travels from the equator, the more the climate cools. The points most distant from the equator, the North and South Poles, are constantly frozen over with ice and are too cold for people to live there. However, various human cultures have long survived in very cool climates that are quite far south and north. Parts of northern Europe and northern Asia, for example, get very cold during the winter, especially in regions with mountains. Ancient cultures that lived in these places faced frozen rivers, streams, and lakes for much of the year, and they used the glassy surfaces to their advantage by turning them into winter roadways navigated on skates. "Before there was *figure* skating," says skating historian and author Ellyn Kestnbaum, "there was skating, on whatever frozen body of water happened to be on hand, an age-old means of transportation."[1]

Ancient skates have been discovered in northern Europe that are about four thousand years old. They were crude devices, fashioned from bones of animals such as elk, reindeer, and oxen. The word *skate*, in fact, comes from the Old English word *schake*, meaning shank or leg bone. People whittled down the bones to taper, or narrow down, at the front and back, then drilled holes in them so that strips of leather or twine could be laced through them and around the wearer's boots. With the bony blades thus attached to their feet, skaters would set out on an icy river or across a frozen

A Saintly Sport

Figure skating may be the only sport in the world with its own patron saint. In 1380 a girl named Lidwina was born in Holland. As a teenager, Lidwina was very religious. Those who knew her felt certain she would become a Catholic nun. One day in 1395, at the age of fifteen, Lidwina's friends talked her into going ice-skating on frozen canals. She had an accident and fell with such force that she broke a rib. Doctors at the time did not know how to treat the injury, and the bone became infected. Lidwina suffered pain and severe complications from the broken bone. She soon became bedridden and stayed so until her death thirty-eight years later, in 1433.

During her time of suffering, Lidwina became even more religious. She slept on a bed of hay because she gave all her possessions to the poor. After her death, people worshipped the memory of her brave life of suffering. In 1890 the Catholic Church named Lidwina the patron saint of skating, and many modern skaters wear her medal.

lake, using handheld branches as poles to propel themselves. Archaeologists in Holland have discovered the skeleton of a man from the Stone Age who died with a pair of horse bones bound to his feet.

Practical though they may have been, Stone Age bone skates left much to be desired. Irregular in shape, rounded or even flat along the bottom edge, and brittle, they gave the wearer little control over balance and direction. In the Middle Ages, people in northern Europe began experimenting with ways to improve skates. First, they replaced bones with blades made out of wood. These could easily be carved into the precise size and shape the wearer wanted. Better still, wood could be waxed on the bottom, which made for faster and smoother gliding across the ice. Then, sometime in the early 1700s, legend has it that a Dutch traveler asked a blacksmith to fashion him a pair of skate blades made out of metal. The blacksmith apparently misunderstood the man's instructions and made the blades narrow along the bottom edge, instead of flat and broad. At first it seemed like an unfortunate error, but when the man tried the thin blades, he discovered they gave him a great deal more stability than the old, broad-bottomed style, and he could maneuver better, too. From that point on, metal skate blades with narrow bottom edges became the most popular kind. The discovery changed the way people skated, because on metal blades, they could make turns and carve interesting designs and "figures" into the ice.

Ice Writing

On metal skates, people discovered artistry in what had previously been only an efficient way to get around in the winter. When a skater gained speed on the new blades and then leaned to the right or the left so that his path curved into a turn, he would carve a majestic arc in the ice behind him. Dutch skaters invented the "Dutch roll," which involved leaning first toward the inside edge of a skate blade and then toward the outside edge, carving a path that arced one direction and then the other. In the 1800s people began competing to see who

Outside Backward.

could make different patterns on the ice. One popular pattern that soon emerged was carving a figure eight, which involved shifting back and forth from the inside edge of the blade to the outside in order to change directions. Doing this on just one foot required balance, grace, and a great deal of practice.

Those who could pull it off were talented skaters, and the more symmetrical and smooth a figure eight they left behind, the better they were deemed to be. Crafting figure eights led to attempting other numbers, letters, and designs. "Writing one's name and drawing elaborate patterns became celebrated feats among accomplished skaters," says Kestnbaum.[2] Winter became a season for skating figures into ice.

Men and women in cold northern climates took up this kind of "figure skating" in growing numbers. Lakes and ponds were filled with skaters testing out their skills. The confined spaces of these often small frozen surfaces required participants to make tighter turns and even to skate backward. They soon began to have friendly competitions to see who could make the smallest turns and draw the most complicated figures in the ice. The English especially took to the idea of skating as competition. They were fascinated with the technical aspect of using skates to make complex patterns, which would pave the way for modern figure skating. "Skating backward and skating circles on smaller radiuses … would prove necessary for later systematic development of techniques of using the body to direct the blades in all the directions it was theoretically possible for them to move," says Kestnbaum.[3] By the mid-1800s figure skating was a deeply entrenched pastime in English society.

While the English were discovering new challenges in figure skating, they also had a great deal of influence on the cultural norms that were evolving for skaters. English society in the 1800s had strict standards as to proper behavior for men and women, and these rules were upheld even when skating. Women, for instance, were required to wear long dresses in public to cover their legs. This convention did not vanish on the ice—female skaters had to skate in their heavy skirts. The men's dress code was not much freer. Gentlemen who wore suits and coats around town wore them on the ice as well. Women and men were also expected to behave properly toward one another while skating and often had separate skating ponds for this reason. Married women were not supposed to dance with men other than their husbands at parties, and for them to skate with other men received disapproval as well. In part because of this social convention, and to the dismay of traditionally minded English men and women, some people began to see a natural connection between skating and dancing.

Skating on Both Sides of the Ocean

While the English were trying to keep men and women apart when skating, an important step in the evolution of skating as dancing on ice occurred on the other side of the Atlantic Ocean. The United States was a newly formed nation with ties to its mother land of England as well as to other European countries from which immigrants came. These people brought a love of figure skating to America, and in northern states where it got cold enough in winter, Americans were carving out their own history in ice. By the Civil War in the 1860s, figure skating and dancing were both very popular in the United States, but most American skaters were practicing the English version of figure skating, with its formal patterns and technical turns. Dancing was considered an entirely separate pastime.

An American named Jackson Haines did much in the 1860s to revolutionize the sport of figure skating by pairing it with dance movements and music. Haines was a trained ballet dancer and teacher who started using a dancer's graceful and athletic movements while on ice-skates. He even set his routines to music. Suddenly, the rigid and stiff practice of carving figures into the ice became something different. Haines flowed and twisted and spun across the ice. "Surprise and astonishment were universal at Haines's first performance," wrote Irving Brokaw, an American figure skater in the late 1800s. "His strokes seem to have been without effort, and his turns were as rapid as lightning. ... In the opinion of those that watched him, not even the most expert dancer on the stage could surpass him in the poetry of motion."[4] Instead of focusing on the shapes of the tracks he left behind, Haines gave people a true performance—an ice dance.

Unfortunately, most Americans were unimpressed with Haines's new style of skating. They preferred the stiff English skating style, which they thought was more proper and masculine for skaters. Haines left North America for France in 1864, where he found crowds that already loved ballet were eager for this new form of dancing on skates. Skaters in France and soon across much of Europe began skating to music and practicing fancy skating maneuvers, like balancing on one leg while soaring across the ice. By the late nineteenth century, skaters and spectators in England and everywhere else were more enchanted with human figures soaring across the ice than with the figures their skates actually *carved* in the ice. "The gracefulness and expressiveness of the skater's movement to the eyes of spectators took precedence," says Kestnbaum, "inspiring skaters to think of what they were doing as dancing on ice."[5] Figure skaters had become performers, forever changing the world of figure skating.

Extending the Skating Season

The more popular this new and showy style of figure skating became, the more people wanted to come out and watch. Skating showed promise of being more than just a fun way for people to pass time in winter. It had turned into a spectator sport. More people than ever wanted to watch or try

Skaters crowd the surface of the first indoor ice rink in London, England, in 1876. John Gamgee's invention of a cooling system that enabled the creation of artificial ice made it possible to skate year-round on a safe, smooth surface.

FIGURE EIGHT

Summer Skaters

The first Olympic figure skating competition was held in summer 1908 on a refrigerated rink during the Olympic Games in London.

figure skating, and not just in colder climates during the winter months. Suddenly there was a demand for ice in balmier southern regions and in the spring, summer, and fall. Inventors found a way to make skating possible anywhere and at any time. In 1876 in London, a British inventor named John Gamgee manufactured the first artificial ice rink, a stadium space with an artificially cooled surface on which water would freeze. As long as the cooling system was working, ice would stay frozen no matter the location or the season.

The invention of artificial ice changed the practice of ice-skating significantly. Not only was the skating pastime now accessible to more people in more places, it was something a person could practice all year. No longer were skaters limited to a few short weeks in winter when ponds and rivers froze naturally. No longer did serious skaters have to travel to the northernmost climates, where winter lasted weeks or months longer and they could spend more time each year practicing their craft. The indoor skating rinks also had safety benefits. In such a rink there was no possibility of skating on ice that was too thin and taking a freezing (and sometimes fatal) plunge into an icy river or pond.

However, the new skating rinks had disadvantages, too. They tended to be small—the earliest rinks measured about 40 feet by 20 feet (12m by 6m), about one-eighth the size of a football field. This was not a lot of room to gain speed for some of the jumps and spins that more and more skaters wanted to try. Furthermore, the rinks tended to be crowded. Even though admission to most early indoor rinks was limited to wealthy members of prestigious skating clubs, thousands of skaters emerged, wanting to try something new and to take part in performances and competitions. Not all who took to the ice were very good at skating, however, so competitive skaters with skill and talent grew irritated by beginners taking up valuable space on the ice. They began to call for rules that would help decide who would be eligible to train in the rinks.

Humanitarian Efforts

In the 1800s skating was a very popular pastime in the United States, especially in Philadelphia, Pennsylvania. The Schuylkill River is a major waterway that runs through the city. It often freezes over in the winter, which made it a very popular skating arena before the days of artificial ice and indoor rinks. Unfortunately, the ice on the Schuylkill was prone to cracking, and skaters sometimes fell through into the freezing-cold water below.

In 1849 a group of gentleman skaters formed the Philadelphia Skating Club and Humane Society. It was mainly an organization to teach figure skating and create interest in the sport, but the club's members—all of them experienced skaters—also helped rescue people who fell through the ice of the Schuylkill River. Members carried a roll of heavy twine with them whenever they were on the ice in the event that a rescue was needed.

Though its members now mostly skate in a huge indoor rink, the Philadelphia Skating Club still exists. With more than one thousand members, it is the oldest and largest skating club in the United States, and a history that marks the spirit of community among skaters.

An illustration shows men, women, and children ice skating on the Schuylkill River in Philadelphia, Pennsylvania, in 1880.

Regulating the Sport

For a long time there were no official regulations about what a skater had to do in order to qualify for real competition. Finally, in 1892, the International Skating Union (ISU) was formed among various nations in Europe. As one of the first official governing bodies for any sport, the ISU made rules for competitive figure skating. It organized the first annual World Figure Skating Championships in 1896, judging participants on their technical merits as well as their artistic presentation. The ISU made it possible for skaters with real talent to set themselves apart from beginners. In order to be eligible for skating competitively, one had to be able to perform a certain number of challenging moves, including jumps and spins.

Skating organizations and their stringent requirements ultimately created a class system among skaters. Whereas skating had once been something anyone in a cold climate could do in winter for fun, space in an indoor skating rink was at a premium. The rinks began to charge large amounts of money for time on the ice. For the most part, only those who could afford admission to the rinks were able to skate year-round, and therefore, to master the skills that the skating organizations required of anyone who wanted to take part in competition. Skating well became a pastime of the wealthy, many of whom did not have to work and could devote themselves to many hours of practice. As skating competitions became more popular worldwide, those who competed in them typically belonged to the upper classes of society. The rules of these organizations forbade competitors to make money at their skating, either through winning cash prizes or getting paid by sponsors to do things like advertise a company's products. It was not possible to make a living at skating, so most who became skaters were already well-off. "Figure skaters were quintessential amateurs," says sports sociologist Mary Louise Adams, "wealthy adults with the money and time to pursue their sport and travel to championships."[6] For decades the average competitive skater was a male from a wealthy family.

Women in the Rink

By the 1900s figure skating had come a long way from its origins, first as a way to get around and then as a way to make fancy drawings in ice. Skaters were developing stunning performances and wowing audiences with their ability to jump, twirl, and dance to music while wearing their skates. Some skaters created moves that were eventually included in the international guidelines, such as the Axel jump invented by Axel Paulsen of Norway in 1882. In this

Norwegian Sonja Henie performs at the 1928 Olympic Games in St. Moritz, Switzerland, the first of three Olympic Games at which she won gold medals. Henie's success and fame increased the sport's popularity among women.

FIGURE EIGHT

Lady Legacy

Sonja Henie is the only woman figure skater ever to win three consecutive Olympic gold medals in the sport—1928, 1932, and 1936.

difficult maneuver, the skater, while moving forward on one foot, pushes off the ice, makes one-and-a-half revolutions, or turns, in the air, and lands on the other foot. Skating routines that included things like Axel jumps were difficult both technically and physically, requiring a great amount of strength. Like most competitive sports, the figure skating rink was considered a man's arena. Perhaps because of the extreme physical demands of skating, no one thought to officially exclude women from competition. Instead, it was just assumed they were not strong enough to master the routines. A young skater named Florence Madeline "Madge" Syers changed that notion when she entered the ISU's world championships in 1902 and finished in second place. The skating community was initially appalled, and the ISU promptly forbade women from entering its competitions. But Madge Syers had made quite a stir in the skating world, and within a few years, in 1906, the ISU allowed women skaters to compete in a ladies' division. Couples' skating was soon introduced, wherein a man and a woman skated their routine together.

In the 1920s, nearly two decades after Syers paved the way for women skaters to succeed, women around the world were experiencing new opportunities. In the United States women had just won the right to vote in political elections. Feeling newly empowered, many American women cut their hair short and learned fleet-footed dances that they performed in short skirts. Called "flappers," these women celebrated freedom from the heavy, long skirts that for generations had been considered the only proper attire for ladies.

It was the perfect time for a beautiful Norwegian named Sonja Henie to make her international skating debut. The ballerina-turned-skater stepped onto the ice in short skirts that not only showed off her legs but allowed her to move freely in her skating routines, unencumbered by a long, heavy skirt. Henie became an international sensation on the ice, winning Olympic gold medals in 1928, 1932, and 1936. "She was truly a force in her sport," says Adams. "Other skaters of the time were impressed by her unique combination of athletic and artistic abilities, her

TAKING HOME THE GOLD

Soviet states **62**

United States **14**

Austria **11**

Canada **10**

Germany **10**

France **9**

Great Britain **6**

China **3**

Belgium **3**

Norway **3**

Sweden **2**

Korea **1**

20

0   5   10   15

Skating Gold Medals 1924 – 2010

* includes Russia, USSR, and Unified Team medals

musicality, her attention to choreography."[7] After winning at three consecutive Olympics, Henie retired from competitive skating to join world ice-skating tours, and she also became a popular American movie star. Largely due to Henie's tremendous success and presence on the ice, female skaters were no longer held back by heavy clothing or social restrictions, and their status on the ice was at last equal to that of men.

Modern-Day Skating

Among men and women alike, figure skating has now become big business for those who excel at it. International regulations finally allow competitive figure skaters to make a living as professional athletes, both by winning prize money in certain competitions and by letting companies sponsor them, or pay them money in exchange for advertising the company and its products. Improved skating rinks with artificial ice have made skating accessible to athletes all around the world (although cooler northern nations such as Russia, Norway, Canada, and the United States still tend to have a far greater number of accomplished skaters than warmer countries closer to the equator).

Even with these changes, skating is sometimes still accused of being an elitist sport. In the United States, where U.S. Figure Skating has regulated skating rules since it formed in 1921, competitors are groomed at an early age through skating clubs that have to follow certain rules. These clubs require young skaters to spend a lot of time on the ice in order to learn the routines and moves they must know to compete. Training to be a skater is expensive and time consuming, and not all athletes and their families (especially those who live far from an indoor rink) can afford the money and time the intensive practice schedules require. Still, the competitive sport of skating is more accessible today than it has ever been, and great skaters truly can come from anywhere, hot or cold, rich or poor.

Unlike other skating sports (such as speed skating and ice hockey), and unlike most competitive sports in general, figure skating is an artistic performance as much as an athletic event. Fans the world over watch in awe as skaters, often in extravagant costumes, execute difficult but beautiful routines to music as they spin and glide across the ice. Few other winter sports compare to figure skating's popularity among fans. By weaving together dancing, music, and physical ability, often with a romantic flair, today's figure skaters transform a simple ice rink into a stage where they can write their own history on the ice.

CHAPTER 2

Physical Properties of Skates and Skating Surfaces

In the four thousand or more years that people have been skating, a lot has changed and improved in the sport. Modern figure skating has evolved into a complex, challenging endeavor that is equal parts athleticism and art form. Rules, guidelines, and social traditions have affected the practice of figure skating over the past several centuries, but certain elements of this pastime have changed very little. Athletes still need skates on their feet that allow them to glide across slick frozen surfaces, for example. Perhaps even more importantly, skaters rely on the one element of skating that has always been present—the ice itself. A scientific understanding of the way ice is formed and how people can cultivate it has made the challenging figure skating routines of modern times possible. Skaters rely on ice's physical properties and the way their skate blades interact with ice in order to create their striking, choreographed movements. In figure skating, the stage for complex and breathtaking performances has always been the frozen form of one of earth's simplest and most abundant chemical compounds: water.

The Chemistry of Water

All things on earth consist of some combination of 117 known chemical elements, each a unique substance that cannot be broken down into anything simpler. One atom of an element such as hydrogen is a microscopic particle and the smallest possible unit of that particular element. Every atom consists of a nucleus at its center, containing particles called protons (which have a positive electrical charge) and neutrons (which have a neutral electrical charge). Orbiting around the nucleus of an atom are electrons, particles that have a negative charge. The positive charge of the protons in the nucleus attracts the negative charge of the electrons orbiting around the nucleus. Atoms of every known element have a unique number of protons and neutrons in the nucleus and electrons orbiting outside the nucleus. This gives each different element its own chemical properties and makes it distinct from all other elements. Every atom of the element hydrogen, for example, has one proton in its

A computer-generated model of water molecules shows white hydrogen atoms bonding to red oxygen atoms, forming hydrogen bonds (yellow lines), resulting in the rigid crystal structure of ice.

nucleus and is usually orbited by one electron. An atom of silver, on the other hand, has 47 protons in its nucleus and is usually orbited by 47 electrons. Their particular numbers of protons, neutrons, and electrons make all elements distinct from one another.

Atoms of the same element sometimes bond together, and so do atoms of different elements. Since positive and negative electrical charges attract each other, the positive charge of the protons in one atom's nucleus sometimes attracts the negatively charged electrons circling another atom. When two or more atoms are attracted to one another, they pull together to form a molecule. Atoms of some elements tend to be strongly attracted to each other or to atoms of certain other elements so

A Job for a Zamboni

Figure skaters can be hard on ice. The blades of their skates constantly carve into the frozen surface, leaving behind tracks and scars that make the ice rough. During skating competitions, the ice must be cleaned and smoothed between performances, or the final skater to compete will unfairly have to perform on rougher ice than his rivals.

The process of resurfacing ice has several steps. First, the ice is scraped or shaved to smooth out rough surfaces. The chunks of scraped ice are swept up and removed. A thin layer of water is then applied to the ice to fill in any holes or cracks that remain, resulting in a smooth surface ready for another performance.

Ice rinks used to be cleaned by crews of workers armed with scrapers, brooms,

and hoses. Cleaning and resurfacing a large rink could take a half-hour. In 1949 a man named Frank Zamboni invented a machine that scraped, swept, cleaned, and re-iced all at once. One of these large machines could resurface a rink in just a few minutes. They became known as Zambonis. Today, the big machines are familiar sights during hockey games, and of course, in figure skating rinks.

A Zamboni machine resurfaces the ice at the 2010 Olympic Games.

that they readily form molecules. The elements hydrogen and oxygen, for example, attract one another. The positive charge of the eight protons in an oxygen atom's nucleus strongly attracts the negative charge of the electrons circling smaller hydrogen atoms. Whenever oxygen and hydrogen share the same space, therefore, they tend to form molecules, each consisting of two hydrogen (H) atoms and one oxygen (O) atom. The resulting molecule is known as H_2O, or water.

Water is one of the most abundant compounds on earth. Approximately 70 percent of the earth's surface is covered by water. At temperatures between 0°C and 100°C (32°F and 212°F), water is in liquid form—the H_2O molecules are loosely bonded, moving around freely and bumping off one another but still staying fairly close together. As the temperature of a substance rises, its molecules move around faster, bumping harder off of one another and not staying as close together. When the temperature of water rises above 100°C (212°F), such as when a pot boils on a stove, the molecules move away from each other and float in the air as a gas, becoming water vapor or steam. On the other hand, when water gets colder than 0°C (32°F), its molecules move around more slowly and do something unusual when they reach their freezing point. "As temperatures get colder, molecules generally move around less vigorously and pack more closely together than at warmer temperatures," says science reporter Mariana Gosnell, "but when water gets cold enough to freeze, the molecules move apart." At water's freezing point, the H_2O molecules form rigid crystals. This solid form of water is known as ice, and its crystal formation makes it less dense than liquid water, so it does something very unique: It floats. "If it did not," says Gosnell, "lakes and seas would freeze from the bottom up."[8] Fortunately for early figure skaters, the unique chemical properties of ice instead created a perfect, floating stage for their sport.

Fast When Frozen

When water freezes into ice, it forms a hard, brittle, and slippery substance, like a hard shell across the top of a river, stream, pond, or lake in climates that get cold in the winter. In the early days of skating, these were the only surfaces on which people could practice. Besides the limited availability of ice, there were other disadvantages to skating on frozen streams or ponds. For one thing, it could be dangerous. Ice is often thicker over some parts of a body of water than others. If a patch of thin ice on a frozen pond or river broke, a skater could fall through into the frigid water below. Another drawback to skating on naturally frozen bodies of water was that the ice was not always a consistent temperature. On a warm day, with the sun beating down directly on the ice, the top layer of ice could heat up enough to start changing back to water. The ice would then be soft, which could make it hard for skaters to get up to speed, since their skate blades would get bogged down in slush.

Yet another problem was that the ice covering frozen rivers, streams, ponds, or lakes did not always have a smooth texture. Bouts of warming and then refreezing could make the surface of the ice rough and choppy, as could the marks left by the blades of other skaters. This rough surface often made it difficult to keep one's balance on skates, and painful or embarrassing falls were common. "On ice that is skated on by many people," wrote nineteenth-century skating enthusiast T. Maxwell Witham in 1897, "a great many long dry cracks appear. … They are most dangerous for the figure skater, for, if in going at a high velocity his skate gets caught longitudinally in one of these, a severe fall is sure to ensue."[9]

Many of these disadvantages were avoided once inventor John Gamgee figured out a way to construct the first artificial ice rink. By the late 1800s serious skaters no longer had to rely on the fickle winter weather for a good time and place to skate. Today, indoor ice-skating rinks are the most common places for figure skaters to practice their skills. These rinks, especially when used for important skating competitions, are constructed and maintained with great care to ensure that the ice is of the highest quality and in the smoothest possible condition for skaters.

Anatomy of a Figure Skating Rink

Water turns to ice when its temperature is lowered to 0°C (32°F) or less. In nature, ice happens when the outdoor temperature surrounding a body of water drops to this

temperature. In an ice rink, however, the ice is not formed by cooling the air *above* a large puddle of water to freezing temperatures. Instead, the ice is formed by cooling the surface *below* the puddle of water until the water freezes, a method Gamgee developed when he invented the first artificially frozen ice. The steps for freezing ice artificially have changed surprisingly little from the early days of manufactured ice. Today's rinks, although bigger and more sophisticated, owe much to their nineteenth-century prototype.

Construction of a skating rink begins with a patch of ground that is covered with a layer of sand and gravel to form a level base. A layer of concrete is poured on top of the base and embedded with tubes to conduct the cooling agent that will be used to lower the temperature of the concrete. Once the concrete has dried and hardened, the pipes running through it are filled with a liquid called brine, which is water with the chemicals calcium and chloride dissolved in it. These added chemicals lower the freezing point of the brine water because their molecules get in the way of the water molecules and make it more difficult for the H_2O molecules

An Olympic-sized figure skating rink, such as this one in Moscow, Russia, may require 10,000 gallons (38,000 liters) of water in order to form the ice surface. The ice is typically created in thin layers that freeze on top of a concrete base cooled by a network of refrigerated pipes.

FIGURE EIGHT

Room to Skate

The world's largest artificial ice rink is the Fujikyo Highland Promenade Rink near the base of Mount Fuji in Japan. It was built in 1967 and covers 165,750 square feet (15,400 sq. meters), or about 3.8 acres.

to form the solid, crystal structure of ice. Brine water remains a liquid at very cold temperatures that would freeze pure water. When the brine water is chilled to a temperature of 16°F (–9°C) and is then pumped continuously through the pipes of the cold concrete layer, the concrete itself becomes cold enough to freeze plain water.

Once cooled, the concrete surface is flooded with water to form layers of ice. The first two to three layers are extremely thin—just 1/32 of an inch (0.08cm). A paint truck drives over the concrete slab, spraying a fine mist of water that freezes almost immediately into each thin sheet of ice. Once the first thin layers are frozen, they can be painted with designs and colors. A final thin layer of ice seals the painted layers. Then a thick layer of ice is created for the skating surface. A flooding hose floods the frozen concrete evenly from end to end, typically using purified water to make sure there are no added chemicals that could later affect the texture and the behavior of the ice. The flooded water is allowed to freeze. This process is repeated over and over until the skating surface reaches the desired thickness. A depth of anywhere from 1 to 3 inches (3cm to 8cm) of ice may be used for figure skating. A greater thickness provides no benefits and only takes more energy to keep frozen.

An Olympic-sized figure skating rink, which is approximately 200 by 100 feet (60m by 30m) in size, may require 10,000 gallons (38,000L) or more of water to be transformed into ice. This volume is applied in layers of 500 to 600 gallons (1,900L to 2,300L) at a time. Freezing multiple thin layers of water one after the other is a process that can take fifteen to twenty hours, but layers of ice added one on top of the other create a stronger and smoother skating surface than if all 10,000 gallons were added at once and left to freeze. Adding all the water in a single layer means the ice could freeze unevenly, creating weak spots, hills and valleys, or cracks in the finished surface. "The thin layers enhance the flatness of the ice surface and also make for a denser sheet," says sports reporter Merrell Noden. "It's absolutely mind-boggling to consider that [the ice slab] is composed of some two dozen distinct layers, built up through repeated floodings."[10]

Regulating the Atmosphere

Once the time-consuming process of making a skating slab is complete, rink engineers take great care to protect the surface of the ice, and they do this by carefully controlling the conditions of the atmosphere inside the rink building. For ice to form naturally outdoors, the air temperature above the body of water must drop below freezing. But because the ice in a skating rink is frozen from underneath, the air temperature in the building does not have to be that cold. In fact, those who build indoor ice rinks have found that the ideal interior air temperature for the building is about 63°F (17°C). This helps to keep the ice surface from becoming either too cold or too warm.

The manager of a skating rink in Bloomington, Minnesota, stands next to an electric-powered refrigeration unit that keeps the building's ice frozen. Creating optimal conditions for competitive skating requires both careful maintenance of the ice surface and monitoring of the building's temperature and humidity levels.

Figure skaters tend to perform best on ice that is 26°F to 28°F (about −4°C). An athlete's skates will dig too deeply into ice that is too warm, creating drag forces on the edges of their skate blades and slowing them down. Ice that is too cold, on the other hand, can prevent the skate blades from digging into the ice at all. Skate blades can slip out from beneath the skaters, causing falls. Ice that is the wrong temperature can also shatter when figure skaters land after jumping. "Figure skating ice is the softest of all Olympic ice surfaces, helping skaters dig in for jumps and spins," explained the Vancouver 2010 International Olympic Committee. "Making great competition ice is not an easy task. It requires the world's top ice makers, known as ice meisters, as well as state-of-the-art ice making equipment and a dedicated team of specialists whose job is to maintain perfect surfaces."[11] In addition to carefully regulated ice surfaces, ice-skating rinks also must have sophisticated heating and air-conditioning units to keep the indoor temperature steady at all times, even if the exterior doors are opened to admit spectators on a warm day.

Humidity is another important factor for indoor ice rinks. Humidity is a measure of the amount of water vapor present in the air. The ideal humidity for an indoor ice rink is about 30 percent. In other words, about a third of the air in the room consists of water vapor. Indoor humidity any greater than 30 percent can create fog over the ice—there is too much water vapor in the air, so the vapor begins to condense into water droplets near the frozen surface. To avoid foggy conditions, indoor ice rinks are equipped with dehumidifiers, machines that remove excess moisture from the air. The temperature and humidity of the air inside the rink and the temperature of the ice itself are constantly monitored when the rink is in use to make sure that skaters can see where they are going and that the ice is the right consistency for the other important physical element of figure skating—the skaters' blades.

Honed for Grace and Speed

The ice of an indoor skating rink is created and tended with great care in order to give skaters a high-quality surface on which to practice their sport. Even the smallest imperfection

A Real Drag

Drag is a force that resists the movement of an object through or across a medium such as air, water, or ice. Drag occurs because a passing object must shove aside the molecules of the medium. In figure skating, skate blades are subjected to drag force because they carve the ice and move its molecules. Too much drag impairs forward speed, but a certain amount of drag helps a skate "grip" the ice when the skater needs to make a sharp turn or push off the ice to begin a jump or spin. Skaters' blades are precisely sharpened to sink in and create drag forces when they are needed or minimize them when they are not.

The ice's temperature also affects drag force. Ice that is nearing its melting point is soft and turns easily to slush. Skaters' blades readily sink into it, increasing drag force and slowing them down. Cold ice is harder, so skates do not sink in. This may improve speed but causes skates to slip if they cannot dig in and create drag forces to abruptly change direction. Skaters, therefore, have distinct preferences about both ice temperature and the sharpness of their blades to take full advantage of drag forces.

in the ice could lead to a botched performance or an injury. The ice is only half of the skater's concern, however. Equally important are the surfaces that must come in contact with the ice in order for skating to happen—the extremely narrow edges of the skater's metal blades.

Figure skating blades have come a long way from the crude prehistoric versions made of wood or bone and strapped with twine to a person's shoes or boots. Modern skates consist of two parts—a leather boot, sized precisely to a skater's foot so that it fits as closely as a glove, and metal skate blades screwed to the bottom of the boot. These metal blades come in a variety of sizes and styles to make all the maneuvers of figure skating possible. The blades are fashioned with extreme precision, using scientific principles from chemistry and mathematics. Each blade is matched

Modern figure skates consist of a leather boot and a metal blade, which can be shaped and sharpened to an individual skater's needs.

perfectly to the individual skater who uses it, with tiny but important changes being made to the way the blade is shaped and sharpened.

The first consideration for a high-quality skating blade is the metal used to make it. Modern blades are made of steel, a mixture of iron and other metals. Some blades are made with stainless steel, a version of steel that is known for being resistant to rusting (a chemical process in which iron, when exposed to water or air, begins to corrode and fall apart). Stainless steel blades are inexpensive to make and to buy, but they have a drawback—the metal is soft, so the skating edges wear down quickly against the surface of the ice and must be sharpened frequently. Most serious skaters, therefore, invest in more expensive blades made from carbon steel. This steel is heated to very high temperatures, which makes it harder than stainless steel so that the skate blades do not dull as easily. Since carbon steel is prone to rusting, the skate blades are usually treated with chrome or nickel through a process called electroplating. In this process they are submerged in a solution of acid and dissolved metal, and when a current of electricity is run through the solution, molecules of the dissolved metal bond to the steel skate blades to form a metallic layer that will help prevent rusting. Because of the extra electroplating process involved in making carbon steel, these skate blades are more expensive, but they are higher quality for skaters who spend many hours on the ice.

The Measure of a Good Skate

Chemistry is not the only thing involved with making great skate blades. Mathematics is also critically important, because it determines the shape and the features of the metal blade. Skate blades are long and slim, measuring anywhere from 7 to 12 inches (18cm to 30cm) long from front to back but as thin as 0.16 inches (4mm) wide along the bottom edge that touches the ice. Learning to balance and maneuver on such a skinny blade can be challenging in itself, but skate blades are also complicated because the bottom edge is not only narrow but curves upward, towards the skater, at the front and back. If one were to stand on the skates, it would be possible to rock slightly from toe to heel. This curved surface of the skate blade is called a rocker.

Geometry is used to determine how much the rocker curves. If the blade was placed flat on the ground and the curve of its rocker were traced, it would form a small section of a larger circle. In any circle, the radius is a measurement of the distance between the midpoint of the circle and its edge. The measure of a skate's rocker is the measurement—usually given in feet—of the radius of the complete circle that would be created if the curve of the rocker were extended into a complete circle. The larger the radius measurement, the larger the circle and the gentler the curve. An 8-foot rocker curve (2.4m), for example, would be less noticeable than a 6-foot rocker curve (1.8m), since a circle with a 6-foot radius would be smaller and the curve therefore more pronounced on the bottom of the skate. "A blade with more rock (a more curved profile) produces cleaner turns but may be more difficult to handle," says Carole Shulman, a professional skating instructor and figure skating judge.[12] The less curved the rocker, the harder it will be to turn, since more

THE HOLLOW OF A SKATE BLADE

The hollow of a skate blade is the indentation that runs along the edge of the blade, made with a grinding wheel, to create two blade edges which dig into the ice and improve the skater's control. The blade's radius of hollow (ROH) refers to the depth of the indentation, which will decrease as the radius of the grinding wheel increases.

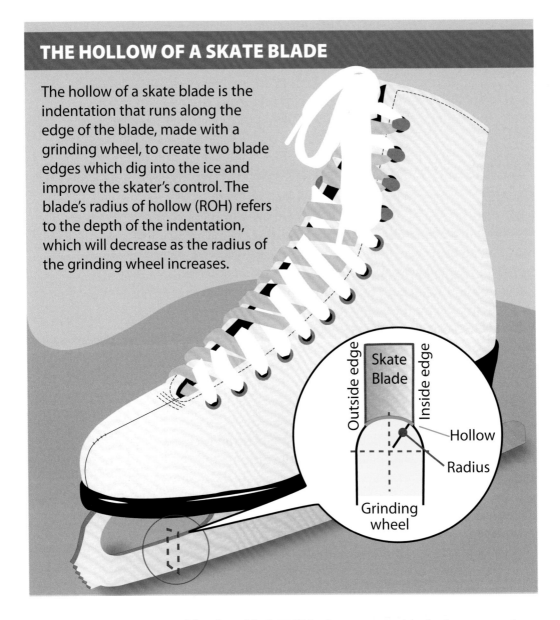

of the skate blade will be in contact with the ice at any given time. However, the skater will have more stability. Different skaters prefer different rocker measurements on their skate blades, based on how experienced they are and how much they like to turn and spin. "The skates must fit according to the skater's age, size, ability, strength, and style," Shulman says. "The skater's goals and potential should also be taken into consideration."[13]

Tragedy Strikes the Skating World

On February 15, 1961, the entire U.S. World Figure Skating Team was aboard Sabena flight 548, going from New York to the World Figure Skating Championships in Prague, Czechoslovakia. The team's plane crashed in a small farming town about 4 miles (6.4km) outside of Brussels, Belgium, killing the seventy-two people on board—all eighteen members of the U.S. team, plus family members, friends, coaches, judges, and officials. The crash, blamed on mechanical problems with the plane, was the worst accident that had ever stricken a sports team.

In the wake of the tragedy, the World Figure Skating Championships were cancelled that year, but U.S. figure skating was crippled for years afterward. Before the crash, the United States had dominated world figure skating, winning the men's gold medal at every Olympics since 1948 and the women's since 1956. After the devastating loss, the United States did not win a women's Olympic gold medal until 1968 and did not win another men's Olympic gold medal until 1984.

A memorial fund was established by U.S. Figure Skating in remembrance of the many lives lost. To this day, the fund still provides skating and academic scholarships to American athletes who show great promise in the sport and have financial need.

Members of the U.S. World Figure Skating Team board the ill-fated Sabena flight 548 on February 15, 1961.

Hollow Quality

The measurement of the rocker is just one factor in choosing a skate blade. Another important element is called the blade's hollow. Skate blades are not flat along their bottom edge. Instead, there is a groove carved into the bottom of the skate blade. This groove is known as a hollow. It creates two edges along the bottom of the blade—an inside edge (toward the inside of the skater's leg) and an outside edge (toward the outside of the skater's leg). The depth of this

FIGURE EIGHT

What a Blade Is Made Of

A magnet will stick to a carbon steel skate blade, but not to a stainless steel one.

hollow in a skate blade can vary greatly, and like the rocker curve the hollow is also measured using geometry and the radius measurement of circles, because a circular honing blade is used to carve the hollow into the base of the skate blade. A tiny honing blade will have a small radius—if the radius is ¼ inch (6mm), for example, the entire honing blade will be just ½ inch (1.3cm) across at its widest point. This blade will create a deeper and more pronounced hollow, or groove, than a honing blade with a bigger radius of 2 inches (5cm).

The size of the groove in the base of a skate blade is called the radius of hollow (ROH). Skate blades with a large ROH will have a bottom surface that is almost flat—the inside and outside edges will be less pronounced. Skates with a small ROH will have a deeper groove in the bottom surface and have very pronounced inside and outside edges. Sharper blades formed by a deeper groove create greater friction, a force of resistance generated when two surfaces, such as the ice and the skate blades, move against each other. A certain amount of friction is necessary when turning on skates, because without it, the blades can slide right out from beneath the skater's body.

The proper ROH ensures each individual skater will get just the right amount of friction from a skate blade during turns. Lightweight skaters, for example, often prefer blades with a smaller ROH, since the more honed edges around the deeper groove will sink deeper into the ice, gripping the ice during turns when skaters' body weight alone might not give them enough friction and grip to turn sharply. Heavier skaters usually prefer a larger ROH, since their body weight causes their skate blades to sink deeper into the ice, and this alone may create enough friction to give their skates plenty of grip. Too little grip can cause a skate to skid during turns, but Shulman says too much grip can also be a disadvantage. "For example," she explains, "the takeoff to a double Axel [jump] almost invariably involves a skid ... and the depth of the hollow greatly influences the length of the skid that can be comfortably made. For this reason, skaters who are used to a certain depth of hollow often lose control of the takeoff edge just after their blades have been sharpened to a slightly deeper hollow."[14] Skaters take great care to choose blades with the perfect ROH for their level of figure skating.

Getting Picky

A final component of modern skate blades is a comb-shaped piece of metal at the toe of the blade. Called a toe rake, it allows skaters to perform many difficult maneuvers on the ice. When the toe rake is tilted downward to scrape against

A skater balances on her toe rakes to hold a pose during a routine. Toe rakes and picks help skaters gain traction to control their speed and push off for jumps and spins.

the ice, it can slow the skater and also give traction for pushing off the ice into a jump or a spin. An especially long tooth at the base of the toe rake has a special name—it is called a toe pick. Jackson Haines, the first-known skater to combine dance moves with skating, is believed to have been the first skater to use toe rakes and picks in order to carry out his dance routines on ice. Even though toe rakes and toe picks are small (the rake is only about ½ inch [1.3cm] long on a typical figure skate), skilled skaters use them all the time when carrying out difficult maneuvers. Just a tiny bit of pressure applied to the toe rake or toe pick can make the difference between a leap and a skid.

The importance of the rocker, the ROH, and the toe rake are evidence of the incredible precision and control skaters must develop as they surge and spin around the ice. Even seemingly tiny particulars in the makeup of the ice and in the structure of the skates can make an enormous difference on the quality and success of a skating performance. Today's figure skaters rely on chemistry and geometry to perfect these small but very important details in order to accomplish the majestic and truly impressive stunts that they learn to carry out on the ice.

CHAPTER 3

The Physics of Figure Skating

O nce the ice is frozen and the skating blades honed to perfection, skaters are ready to take to the rink, carrying out phenomenal stunts of balance, strength, and finesse on a slippery surface gripped only with metal blades 1/4 inch (0.6cm) wide. As they soar across the ice, spin at dizzying speeds, and launch themselves into twirling jumps, these athletes strive for technical perfection and unique artistic flair that will stand out among competitors all trying to put on the most entertaining show of the day. Figure skaters are judged by whether they include all the required moves during a two- to five-minute routine and with how much precision they accomplish them. Meeting the judges' stiff criteria requires mastery of the rules of physics—the science of matter and how it moves. Skaters rely on concepts like velocity, inertia, and momentum to carry out their complex routines.

Skating for Speed

Long before attempting jumps and spins, a skater must move either forward or backward. When standing on the ice on a pair of skates, he is subject to the first basic law of physics, as described by scientist Sir Isaac Newton in 1687. Newton observed that any object at rest (not moving) will stay at

A skater glides forward across the ice as a result of Newton's law of motion, which is enacted when he uses his leg muscles to push his blades against the ice.

rest unless some force acts on it to make it move. To go anywhere, therefore, a skater must apply force against the ice. He angles his skate blades so their edges dig in, bends his knees, and uses the muscles in his legs to push his skates against the ice. As he does so, he relies on another law of motion described by Newton: Every action (such as pushing one's skates against the ice) has an equal and opposite reaction (the ice, in turn, pushes against the skates). "At each foot contact," explain kinesiologists William Charles Whiting and

Stuart Rugg, "the force that the foot exerts on the ground is equally and oppositely resisted by the ground."[15] The skater pushes, the ice pushes back, and the skater glides forward.

An important physical phenomenon that affects a figure skater, both standing still and in motion, is inertia. The skater's body is made of matter (which is anything that can be physically touched), and anything made of matter has mass, or a measure of the amount of matter in an object of a certain size. Any body that has mass also has inertia, which means it will resist any change in its state of motion. Initially, the nonmoving skater's inertia causes him to remain still. Once he supplies force by pushing against the ice with his legs, the ice (which has inertia, too, and wants to remain still) pushes in the opposite direction. This causes the skater to start moving. He has velocity, or a speed at which his body is changing its position on the ice. He also has momentum, a measure of motion that depends on the mass of his body and the velocity at which he is moving. The skater still has inertia as well—now that he is moving in one direction, his body will resist any changes in that state of movement unless another force is applied.

One force that can affect a moving skater's inertia is friction, the force of resistance created when two surfaces, such as the ice and the skates, move against each other. "A skater glides across the ice until the friction between the skate and the ice eventually brings him to a stop," say Whiting and Rugg.[16] But ice is slippery and skates slide easily on it, so the force of friction may not be strong enough to stop the skater before he runs out of ice to skate across. He must apply force to either stop moving or to change the direction of his movement before he careens into the wall of the ice rink. To change direction, he has to turn.

Skating in Circles

Rarely do figure skaters move very long in a perfectly straight line. Gliding straight across the rink would not make a very interesting performance. Skaters instead dig the edges of their skates into the ice to make turns. These turns are done in lobes, or half circles, due to the shape of the figure skater's

A skater leans on the outside edge of her left skate blade in order to make a turn during her routine. A skater's ability to turn in a particular direction and carve lobes into the ice is governed by Newton's laws of motion.

blade. The radius of hollow (ROH), the groove cut into the base of a skating blade, gives the blade two distinct edges—the inside edge, toward the inside of the leg, and the outside edge, toward the outside of the leg. A skater usually has just one foot and leg on the ice at a time, known as the skating leg. The other (the free leg) is preparing to take the next skating step, or it may be held out in front of or behind the skater as she glides on one foot. If the skater leans toward one side of the skating leg, the blade will lean onto a single

Voice of the Ice

In the 1940s and 1950s Dick Button was the best male figure skater in the world. Winner of seven straight U.S. championships and five world championships, Button also won Olympic gold medals in 1948 and 1952. He was the first skater to land a double Axel jump or a triple loop jump in competition. In 1960, after retiring from competitive skating, Button returned to the Olympic arena—this time as a commentator. He closely analyzed the performances of the Olympic skaters at Squaw Valley, California, and gave honest, if sometimes harsh, explanations of what the skaters had done right and wrong. During that Olympic tournament and at every one since, Button helped television viewers understand what was happening on the ice and why skaters received the scores they did.

Now in his eighties, Button has been the voice of Olympic figure skating for more than five decades. He no longer skates, after suffering a terrible skating accident in 1990 that fractured his skull and left him deaf in one ear, but his reputation as one of the best figure skaters of all time gives credibility to his criticism of skaters. As both a skater and a commentator, Button has helped shape the modern world of figure skating in more ways than one.

edge and the skater will begin a turn in the shape of a lobe. Skaters lean their body in the direction that they wish to turn, and this will tilt their weight to the proper edge of the skating foot in order to make the turn.

The reason leaning onto a certain edge of the skate blade results in a turn also has to do with the laws of physics developed by Isaac Newton. Since the skater's moving body has inertia, its natural tendency is to continue to travel in a straight line in whatever direction it is already going. Tilting onto one edge of a skate blade, however, makes that edge cut into the ice. The skater is applying a new force to the ice, so the ice pushes back in the opposite direction. If the skater leans to the right, the blade edge digs in and exerts pressure in a leftward direction. The ice "pushes" back, nudging the skater the opposite way—to the right. The amount of force she applies to the edge of the skate will determine whether the lobe is small or wide: The harder the skater leans on the edge, the more force the blade will exert and the more force the ice will exert back, so the faster she will turn and the tighter the lobe will be.

Though most spectators focus on the jumps and spins of figure skating, edges and turning on curves are the important first skills that any skater masters on the ice. "In skating today, a great deal of emphasis is placed on jumping, spinning, and big tricks," says Nancy Kerrigan, an Olympic silver medalist in figure skating. "However, skating is more than jumping, spinning, and lifting. Watching a truly gifted artistic skater … removes all doubt that it is not only what they do with their bodies in the air that makes them great but also the patterns they leave behind on the ice."[17] Such patterns are made with the eight different edges, or turns, possible in figure skating. There are a right and a left forward outside edge (the skater is moving forward on the right or left foot and leaning to the outside of the skating foot); a right and a left forward inside edge (the skater is moving forward and leaning to the inside of the skating foot); a right and a left backward outside edge (the skater is moving backward and leaning to the outside of the skating foot); and a right and left backward inside edge (the skater is moving backward and leaning to the inside of the skating foot). Mastering these edges and the curves they make is fundamental before moving on to other moves: the spirals, spins, and jumps that make the sport of figure skating so entertaining.

Graceful Spirals

Although carving lobes into the ice using the principles of physics is quite technical, figure skaters also specialize in performance art and drama. Soon after mastering the basics of moving forward and backward and using one's edges to change direction in curves, skaters learn moves that are graceful and entertaining to watch. Spirals are one such maneuver. The skater pushes off the ice to gain momentum.

To perform a spiral, a skater uses almost all of the muscles in her body to maintain a position that will optimize the effects of gravity and maintain balance.

Then she balances on one skate while lifting her free leg into the air, usually extending it behind her as she glides across the ice.

Almost every muscle in the skater's body is used to maintain balance during a spiral. The body's natural tendency is to fall over in spiral position because of something called center of gravity. "Every body contains a point, known as the center of gravity, about which that body's mass is evenly distributed," say Whiting and Rugg.[18] This is the one point within any object, the human body included, where its total

Ice Queen

Every now and then an athlete leaves a special mark on his or her sport. In figure skating, one such athlete is Michelle Kwan. Born in California in 1980 to a Chinese American family, Kwan spent her early years watching an older brother play hockey. She took up skating at age five and won her first competition at age seven. By the time Kwan was a teenager, the whole world knew her name. She won forty-two championships in her career, including five World Championships and eight consecutive U.S. Championship titles from 1998 to 2005—something no other U.S. skater has done. The one award that eluded Kwan was an Olympic gold medal—she won a silver and a bronze, but never topped the podium. That mattered little to her millions of young admirers, who gave her Kids' Choice and Teens' Choice Awards as America's favorite female athlete of 2002 and 2003. She was also named one of *People* magazine's fifty most beautiful people in 2000. Kwan is the most decorated figure skater in U.S. history and received fifty-seven perfect 6.0 marks in major competitions, the most of any singles skater ever. Though now retired from skating, Kwan has left her mark on the ice.

Kwan waves to the crowd from the medals podium after her win at the U.S. Figure Skating Championship in 2004.

weight is perfectly balanced. If the object were set on top of a pole or a stick at its exact center of gravity, it would not topple over. Objects of different shapes have different centers of gravity. In people, say Whiting and Rugg, "The center of gravity normally is located along the body's midline,"[19] approximately at a person's navel. The closer a person's limbs are to his or her center of gravity, the easier it is to balance. When one leg is extended away from the body, as in a spiral, the skater's torso, the upper half of her body, must lean forward, acting as a counterbalance to the weight of the leg so that her center of gravity continues to balance over the single skate blade remaining on the ice. The skater uses muscles in her stomach, back, arms, and legs to hold her body in a spiral position. Leaning too far in any direction will make her lose her balance, so her muscles constantly make tiny adjustments to hold her posture upright. This control and attention to detail is a key skill for all figure skaters. "Good posture is necessary in all skating disciplines," explains Kerrigan. "Skaters need to stand … with the chest and head lifted and the abdominal muscles controlled."[20]

There are many different types of spirals. Some skaters, such as Kerrigan, like to hold on to the extended knee with one hand, while others may hold both arms out to the sides during a spiral. Some skaters are flexible enough to raise their leg straight in back of them and hold it behind their head with both hands. Others lean forward so far that they can hold on to the ankle of their skating leg during a spiral. Whatever its style, a spiral is an intense, difficult skating maneuver that requires concentration, strength, and mastery of one's balance and center of gravity.

Stunning Spins

During a spiral, the skater glides across the ice in a forward or backward direction while extending one leg. This kind of movement is called linear motion—the skater moves along either a straight line or, in the case of skating in lobes, a curved one. A second type of maneuver, the spin, is another required element of competitive skating, but one in which the skater makes no forward or backward movement across the ice. Instead, he uses a kind of movement called angular, or rotational, motion. He spins around an axis of rotation, an imaginary vertical line through his center of gravity.

INCREASING ROTATIONAL VELOCITY DURING SPINS

Increasing a spinning object's radius will decrease its velocity and increase its moment of inertia, or potential for movement. A spinning skater with outstretched arms has a greater radius from their center of rotation, and drawing in the arms can decrease the body's radius and increase rotational velocity. Skaters often begin a spin with open arms or a leg out, then pull their limbs in to create a long, dazzling spin.

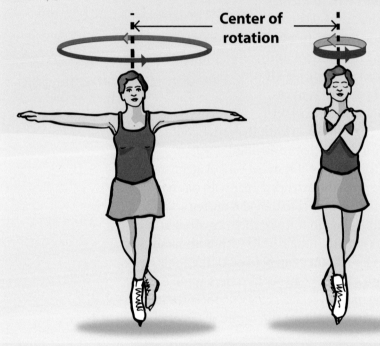

Center of rotation

One challenge of spinning maneuvers in skating is that they require as much velocity, or speed, as linear maneuvers. In fact, a skater's spins are judged in part by how fast he rotates and how many revolutions, or full turns, he makes during the spin. A skater must build linear momentum and velocity before going into the spin, which he does by pushing against the ice with his edges, one foot after the other. The skater converts linear momentum and velocity into angular (rotational) momentum and velocity by twisting his arms, upper body, and weight-bearing leg in the direction he wants to spin. This swings his body, which has linear momentum, into a spinning motion with angular momentum.

Good skaters do not merely spin once or twice around a fixed point until they lose speed. They actually can spin faster and faster once they change linear momentum to angular momentum. They are able to do this because of a physics concept called the moment of inertia, which is a measurement of a spinning object's resistance to a change in its spinning motion. Just as with linear inertia, in which a moving object

A skater performing a spin move positions her arms and legs close to the center of her body in order to decrease her moment of inertia and increase the speed at which she rotates.

will continue moving until friction or other forces slow it down, a spinning object will not stop spinning unless through a force like friction. A spinning skater's moment of inertia is greater—it takes more energy to keep him spinning—if his arms and legs are extended from his body than if he pulls them in tightly. This is because his weight is distributed over a larger area if his arms and legs are outstretched—the energy and momentum of his spinning body are spread out over more space, so his body turns more slowly. Pulling his outstretched arms in to his torso will decrease the skater's moment of inertia—the same amount of energy and momentum are in the spin, but there is less body area spread out far from the axis of rotation, so the speed of the spin increases. "If the moment of inertia decreases but the angular momentum stays constant," says chemist and science writer Steve Miller, "the rate of motion must increase. As the skater brings her arms in, she spins faster and faster, going from about 2 rotations per second to 10 or more rotations per second."[21] Figure skaters achieve dizzying speeds during their spins when they pull their arms and legs tight to their body.

There are many types of spinning maneuvers in skating. In upright spins the skater stands, usually on just one foot, and spins either clockwise or counterclockwise while holding the arms and the free leg tight to the center of his body. Skaters also perform sitting spins, where they spin while squatting down on one leg and extending the other leg out in front of them. Once they are done with a spinning maneuver, skaters outstretch their arms again to raise the moment of inertia and slow the spin so they can gracefully begin a different move. "Spinning fast makes it difficult to control oneself," says physics professor John Eric Goff. "Skaters are not spinning during their entire routines."[22] Instead, they mix spins with spirals and a third technical element required in figure skating routines—jumps.

Daring Jumps

Spins and spirals take practice, flexibility, and a great understanding of physics, but jumps are the most difficult maneuvers for most skaters to master. A jump on skates requires

a combination of other skating skills. The skater must first generate great speed for the jump. She then balances on one leg and extends her free leg out behind her to prepare for the extreme physical effort the jump will require. The free leg will actually create torque in the skater's body, a twisting force that causes rotation. As she pushes off the ice with her skating leg to begin the jump, the skater draws her extended leg in and twists her torso, trying to generate enough torque to spin her body at least one whole revolution in midair before she comes back down to the ice. Spinning in the air during a jump is similar to spinning on ice in that the arms and the free leg are drawn in toward the body's axis of rotation to increase speed in the spin. The jump is vastly different, however, in that the skater must keep track of how many revolutions she has made and how soon she will be drawn back down to the ice by gravity—the force that attracts a body toward the earth. If she waits too long to position her body for landing, she will fall, possibly hurting herself and almost certainly ruining her chances of a high score from the judges.

From right to left, skater Surya Bonaly moves through the phases of a jump, which requires her to master both horizontal and vertical momentum as well as torque in order to make her body spin.

Technical Twirls

The seven kinds of jumps in figure skating routines differ based on the direction the skater is moving going into the jump (forward or backward), the leg the skater takes off from and lands on, and whether or not the toe pick at the front of the skate blade is used. One of the simpler jumps is the waltz, where the skater begins by skating a curved path forward or backward on the outside edge of one skate, jumps and turns in the air, and lands on the outside edge of the other skating foot. A more difficult variation of this jump is the Axel, invented by skater Axel Paulsen in 1882. To perform a single Axel, the skater glides forward on the outside edge of one skate, then leaps into the air, completing one and a half rotations in order to land on the outside edge of the opposite foot gliding backward.

In loop jumps, the skater takes off and lands on the same foot instead of changing feet during the jump. A basic loop jump begins with the skater gliding backward on an outside edge, leaping and rotating once in the air, and landing on the outside edge of the same foot, still gliding backward. A toe loop jump is carried out much the same way, but at the start of the jump, the skater uses the toe pick of the free leg to kick off the ice, gaining speed and height. Like a loop jump, the takeoff and landing are on the same leg, with the skate on an outside edge.

To perform a Salchow jump, invented in 1909 by Swedish skater Ulrich Salchow, a skater glides backward on the inside edge of one foot, makes a complete revolution in the air, and lands the jump on the outside edge of the opposite foot, gliding backward. A flip jump is similar to a Salchow, but the skater uses the toe pick of the free leg at the start of the jump to launch higher into the air.

The final type of figure skating jump is the lutz. The skater usually begins on the left foot, moving backward in a wide arc on the skate's outside edge (thus, leaning to his left). He stretches his free right leg behind him, then pulls it sharply forward, using the toe pick to scrape the ice and push off into the jump. In midair, the skater twists his body opposite of the way he was leaning—he was leaning hard to his left but jumps toward his right, changing legs during the jump to land on the outside edge of his right foot. It takes great strength and skill to overcome a strong leftward lean and push off into a rightward rotation, making the lutz a very difficult jump for most skaters. Like any other jump, a lutz is made even more difficult if the skater adds rotations in the air to achieve a double, triple, or even quadruple jump.

Jumps in figure skating are more complex than other maneuvers because they require different kinds of momentum. At the start of the jump the skater already has horizontal momentum, or movement along the surface of the ice, because she has been pushing her skate blades against the ice to create speed. To complete a jump, she will also have to use her body's muscles to create vertical momentum, or movement straight up in the air. If there were only horizontal momentum, the skater would never leave the surface of the ice. If there were only vertical momentum, the skater would jump straight up and come straight down but would not have the forward (horizontal) momentum needed to complete revolutions in midair. A skater's path during a jump takes the shape of a parabola, like the shape of a bell. If her center of gravity, approximately her belly button, could draw an imaginary line in the air during her jump, it would start parallel to the ice surface (horizontal momentum), rise into the air (vertical momentum), crest, slope back down as the skater returned to the ice, and end parallel to the ice surface again as she landed the jump. "Jumping—the result of a combination of speed, timing, power, distance, flow, and finesse—is like being on a roller coaster," says Elvis Stojko, a world champion figure skater and Olympic silver medalist. "Momentum swiftly hoists you up and then plunges you down, before you can catch your breath."[23]

There are six different types of jumps in figure skating, depending on whether the skater pushes off from the edge or the toe pick of the skate blade and whether he is moving on a forward or a backward edge going into the jump. The jumps include the Salchow, invented by Swedish skating champion Ulrich Salchow in the early 1900s, and the Axel, named after Norwegian figure skater Axel Paulsen, who invented the jump in 1882. Loops, toe loops, flips, waltzes, and lutzes are the other styles. Any jump can involve one, two, three, or even four full revolutions of the skater's body while in the air, marking the difference between a single lutz (one revolution before landing), for example, and a quadruple lutz (four revolutions).

FIGURE EIGHT
A Star's Rise and Fall

Tonya Harding was the first U.S. woman to land a triple Axel jump in a figure skating competition. She was later banned for life from competitive skating due to her role in an attack on her teammate, Nancy Kerrigan.

A quadruple jump, if performed and landed correctly, gets the most points from the judges because it is very difficult, requiring more time in the air to complete all the revolutions. The skater must build greater velocity leading up to the jump, greater vertical momentum as the skating leg pushes off the ice, and greater spinning speed in the air to complete more revolutions. The added speed, height, and spinning rate of these jumps also make them very hard to land on just one foot. Many skaters are intimidated by jumps with multiple revolutions. "It (a quadruple) takes a different mind-set than the other jumps," says Timothy Goebel, Olympic bronze medalist and former U.S. national figure skating champion. "Whether you land a quad or not, it can set the tone for the rest of the program."[24] The quadruple Axel is considered the most difficult maneuver in figure skating, and no known skater to date has been able to land one. Professional skaters often do, however, attempt double and triple Axels, and even quadruples of other jumps, in their quest to outperform their competition.

Coupled Up

All figure skaters strive to incorporate spirals, spins, and jumps gracefully into their routines, but some skaters have additional requirements in their programs. These are pairs skaters, a man and woman who skate together as a couple. Like single skaters, pairs skaters are expected to include spirals, spins, and jumps in their routines, but they have the added challenge of synchronizing these movements, or completing them at the exact same speed, same time, and in the same direction. In addition, pairs skaters have other elements they must incorporate into their programs. These include daring moves like throw jumps, in which the man spins the woman into the air by her waist and one hand so she can achieve more height during a jump, and overhead lifts, in which the man must lift his partner into the air and carry her, balanced over his head, as he skates. "Pairs skating combines all of the elements of singles skating with another person to create overhead lifts, spins, and jumps unique to the discipline," says Kerrigan. "However, unlike the other

[skating] disciplines, pairs skating has another element of danger that thrills the spectator."[25]

As with all skating maneuvers, controlling the center of gravity is essential for both skaters if moves such as overhead lifts are to be a success. During a lift, the man's body forms a solid base for the woman's as he holds her above his head. If he is even a little off balance, they both will topple over. The woman, while being held high in the air, must keep her own center of gravity stable and in line with the man's. If she tilts too far, she or both of them will fall. Skating as a couple often takes even more strength, balance, control, precision, and practice than singles skating. "Pairs skating is definitely not for the faint of heart," says Kerrigan, but "it can be exhilarating to watch and a joy to participate in."[26]

Pairs skating demonstrates the beauty of figure skating as an art form and also the great strength and physical fitness necessary to carry out the difficult physical maneuvers the sport demands. Jumps, spins, lifts, and other skating movements require not just a mastery of body mechanics but a great deal of strength and control of the body's many muscles. All skaters, whether they skate individually or in pairs, must make sure the physical conditioning of their body is equal to the task, not just to perform well in competition but to prevent the serious injuries this sport can cause.

CHAPTER 4

Fitness and Injuries in Figure Skating

On October 31, 1999, at the Skate America competition in Colorado Springs, Colorado, Timothy Goebel made figure skating history. In a skating program lasting 4.5 minutes, he landed three quadruple jumps, something no other skater in the world had done before. His accomplishment came just one year after he became the first American man to land any quadruple jump in competition, which earned him the nickname "Quad King." Pulling off three quadruple jumps in less than five minutes in a single skating routine, in addition to seven triple jumps, demonstrated a level of physical fitness that was nothing short of incredible to spectators and to Goebel's competitors that day. "This unbelievable accomplishment illustrates the future of skating and the technical prowess that skaters must achieve to become national, world, and Olympic contenders," says professional skating instructor and judge Carole Shulman.[27]

Goebel's success raised the bar for elite skating athletes, who pursue athletic feats that seem to require almost superhuman strength. Skaters regularly attempt difficult quad jumps, triples, and back-to-back jump combinations. These require incredible power and endurance. To accomplish such feats, figure skaters do much more in their training than just skating for hours each day to master technical moves. In addition to practicing their complicated and difficult routines, they must develop strength and flexibility that surpass almost any other sport if they are to keep up with the best skaters in the world and avoid getting hurt. "Figure skaters have gradually expanded off-ice training in order to enhance overall conditioning and performance and to decrease training time lost to injury," says physician J.M. Moran. "Off-ice conditioning must be incorporated into the training [program]."[28] Many figure skating athletes do as much training in sneakers as on skates to develop the muscle strength the sport demands.

Powering a Skating Routine

The various moves required in figure skating programs—such as spirals, spins, and jumps—require the body to be in nearly constant motion. This is accomplished by pushing against the ice to build momentum, overcome inertia, and

A side view of the muscles of the human hip and thigh shows the hamstrings on the left, behind the femur, and the quadriceps on the right, on top of the femur and above the knee joint. These muscles work together to power a skater through a routine.

Traveling Talent

Figure skaters are performers, not just athletes, and traveling ice-skating shows have long been a popular venue where skaters can continue to entertain crowds after retiring from competition. The Ice Capades, founded in 1940, was one such traveling show. Over the years, it featured many of America's most famous competitive skaters, including Olympic gold medalists Dick Button, Dorothy Hamill, Peggy Fleming, and Scott Hamilton, all of whom toured with the Ice Capades after retiring from their Olympic careers. The show allowed the American public a chance to see favorite Olympic stars perform in person. The Ice Capades were popular for five decades, but in 1994, the long-running show finally came to an end. Other traveling shows like Holiday on Ice and a children's favorite, Disney on Ice, have since helped fill the demand for figure skating. Reality TV even took a turn around the rink with its 2010 show *Skating with the Stars*, pairing celebrities with professional skaters for a viewer-judged season of ice competition. Professional skaters stay famous with such appearances and make money doing what they love, while fans of figure skating do not have to wait four years between Olympics to watch their favorite sport.

in the case of jumping, defy the constant force of gravity that pulls everything with mass close to the earth. The body's muscles provide the energy for these kinds of movements. Muscles are the powerhouses of the body, and for a skater, building and maintaining strong muscles are essential to creating and carrying out the kinds of performances that will impress judges and beat competitors.

Muscles are part of the body's musculoskeletal system, the organ system that carries out movement. The bones of the body (the skeletal system) protect internal organs and also provide structure, shape, and support so people can sit or stand. Muscles attach to the bones and work to pull them in specific ways so the body can perform movements such

FIGURE EIGHT

Full Force

Figure skaters land their jumps with a force 10 to 12 times their body weight. Runners' feet strike the ground with a force of only about 3 times their body weight.

as walking, raising the arms, bending over, or turning the head. Muscles consist of clusters of fibers that can stretch and contract. They work something like clumps of rubber bands. When they contract, they pull on the bone they are attached to, moving it in one direction. Major bones in the body, such as the long bones of the arms and legs, all have muscles attached to them. Because muscles, when contracted, pull bones in just one direction, they are paired with muscles that will pull the bone in the opposite direction. For example, the quadriceps muscle is a large muscle that runs along the front of the femur, the big bone in the thigh. The hamstring muscle runs along the back of the femur. When the hamstring contracts, it pulls the lower leg back at the knee joint and stretches the quadriceps. When the quadriceps contracts, it pulls the lower leg forward at the knee joint, and the hamstring stretches. Muscles throughout the body work in similar pairs. Skaters rely on these pairings of muscles to carry out all their movements on the ice. The stronger and more developed their muscles, the better skaters' performances will be, so their off-ice training programs concentrate on building the different types of muscle strength they will need.

Training for Strength

One type of strength that is important to skaters is called maximal strength. This is the maximum amount of force that a muscle can produce in a single contraction, without relaxing or resting in between movements. Increasing a muscle's maximal strength will increase the amount of height that a skater can get out of a jump, for example, as she uses that muscle to push off of the ice. It will also extend the amount of time the skater will be able to contract muscles. For example, to hold a spiral position, the gluteal muscles that make up the buttocks need maximal strength so the skater

can keep one leg extended to the rear without lowering it to rest. Pairs skaters rely a great deal on maximal strength. The male skater of the pair must be able to contract his muscles to lift the female skater overhead and then hold her in that position. Most skaters spend time lifting weights to increase their maximal strength so they can jump higher and hold difficult positions longer. To do so, they concentrate on lifting a certain amount of weight (such as 15 pounds [7kg]) a certain number of times (such as 10 repetitions) to complete an exercise set.

During weight training, skaters usually complete three sets of a certain number of repetitions of a certain weight for each muscle they are working on. Lifting heavier weights, using fewer repetitions, and taking several minutes of rest in between sets will help build bigger muscles that can do more explosive movements, like sudden jumps. Any time muscles are slightly overused, or forced to work a little harder than what they are used to, the muscle tissue forms tiny tears. When the body repairs these tears over the following days, it also reinforces the muscle tissue, making it stronger and

Skater Philippe Candeloro works out with weights in order to optimize his maximal strength, which is key to skaters achieving height in their jumps and hold a spiral or spin position.

more resilient than before. Over time, weight training builds stronger muscles capable of lifting more weight and holding it for a longer time. This is the goal of weight training programs for skaters—they are building improved bodies with stronger muscles that will let them skate better routines.

Training for Endurance

Lifting heavy weights and resting in between sets helps to make muscles bulkier and more capable of hoisting one's body (or one's partner, in the case of pairs skating) into the air. Sheer lifting power is not all a skater's muscles must be able to do, however. Lifting lighter weights with more repetitions and short rests in between will enhance the muscles' ability to keep working hard for a long time without tiring and losing strength. This is called muscle endurance, and it is just as important to a skater as maximal strength. A skater who has focused on maximal strength alone may be able to lift himself high into the air for an incredible jump, but if he

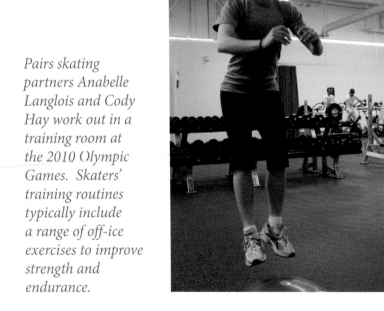

Pairs skating partners Anabelle Langlois and Cody Hay work out in a training room at the 2010 Olympic Games. Skaters' training routines typically include a range of off-ice exercises to improve strength and endurance.

has tired his muscles out after that one maneuver, he will not be able to skate the rest of his routine with skill and grace. Skaters like Goebel have the maximal strength to complete an impressive jump and also the endurance to complete several more jumps in addition to spins and spirals. Skaters train off the ice for muscle endurance by doing activities like running, swimming, and bicycling to get their muscles used to working hard even when tired. "This is a total-body sport," says Olympic sports columnist Ron C. Judd, "and the same types of training techniques—running, resistance and weight training, and reflex drills—used by other athletes have found their way into the modern figure skater's training quiver. Some top skaters also devote many hours to formal dance training and other pursuits bordering more on art than athleticism; it is necessary, they say, to become a complete skater, balancing fluidity with power."[29]

Different skaters need different strength-training programs, depending on what they are currently good at and what weaknesses they are trying to correct. Strength coaches design unique training programs for each skater, focusing on what a particular athlete most needs to accomplish. Some skaters might get tired during their routines, for example, and they might need strength training that focuses on endurance. Other skaters might have trouble holding a spiral position and might need help developing maximal strength in the muscles of the legs and the abdomen. Because muscles work in pairs, strength trainers make sure that athletes are not developing one strong muscle of a pair (such as the quadriceps muscle) while neglecting the other muscle of the pair (the hamstring). This could create an imbalanced body where the strong quadriceps pulls harder than the hamstring can withstand, which in turn could injure the hamstring or the knee joint. In short, a skater's strength-training program is as unique as the skater herself.

Stretching for Gold

Just as important as having strong muscles is having flexible ones. Flexibility is a measure of how well a person can move the parts of his or her body around joints—the places

Michelle Kwan does a stretching routine prior to her performance at the 2002 Olympic Games. Stretching increases a skater's flexibility, which results in a greater range of motion, graceful movements, and resistance to injury.

where two or more bones come together. Flexible athletes have muscles that can stretch easily. Athletes who have poor flexibility cannot do things like bend at the hip to touch their toes or stretch one leg straight up to the side. Flexibility is a critical component of muscle fitness, especially for athletes like figure skaters whose performances depend on a large range of motion from muscles that can move fluidly. The world's best skaters are generally able to achieve back bends, hoist one foot up to shoulder height, and make sweeping movements with their arms, legs, and torso. Flexibility training not only makes for graceful skating performances, it also creates loose, pliable muscles that are more resistant to injuries during strenuous skating routines.

Skaters increase flexibility by stretching their muscles often and thoroughly. Skaters may spend twenty minutes or more during each practice session sitting or standing on a floor mat and moving through stretching exercises that target every major muscle in the body—the hamstrings, the quadriceps, the calves of the legs, and the muscles of the arms, back, and neck. Stretching exercises work to pull on and lengthen the fibers of the muscles to keep them from being tightly

Salt Lake City Scandal

At the time of the 2002 Winter Olympics in Salt Lake City, Utah, Russian pair-skating teams had won gold at every Olympic tournament since 1964. When scores for the 2002 pair-skating event came in and Russians Elena Berezhnaya and Anton Sikharulidze were in first place, it should have been no surprise—except for the fact that the Russians truly had not skated the best program. Even people at home watching on TV thought the Canadian team, Jamie Sale and David Pelletier, had skated flawlessly, while the Russians had made obvious technical errors. Public outcry raised questions about biased skating judges, and during the investigation that followed, a French judge admitted she had been pressured to cast her first-place vote for the Russians. Sale and Pelletier were given gold medals to replace silver. Berezhnaya and Sikharulidze were allowed to keep their gold medals as well. The 2002 Winter Games went down in history as a rare event in which four athletes tied for gold. The scandal brought about major changes in the way figure skating is scored, making it far less likely that a judge can be pressured or bribed into changing the outcome of a competition.

Pelletier and Sale, left, and Sikharulidze and Berezhnaya pose with their gold medals at the 2002 Olympic Games.

contracted all the time. "Stretching can also improve posture, which, in turn, improves performance and enhances presentation," Shulman says. "Exceptional levels of flexibility are required for spirals, split jumps, … spins, and pair and dance moves."[30] Muscles that are not flexible may also have a hard time contracting to perform a sudden movement, so flexibility even increases muscle strength and performance.

Training in Moderation

Without strong and flexible muscles, no one could withstand the intense physical activity required by competitive figure skating. Whole-body fitness, including strength, endurance,

The performance of a pairs skating team is optimized if the female partner can maintain a lean body composition in contrast to her male partner, who needs more muscular bulk in order to have the strength to skillfully and safely complete a routine.

and flexibility, are absolutely essential for figure skating. These athletes spend many hours off the ice every week lifting weights and doing other exercises designed to build strong, pliable muscles capable of withstanding the physical demands of the rink. Skaters must take care not to overdo their muscle building, however. They strive for what is called optimal strength—a point at which they are strong enough to do everything their routines call for, but where getting stronger and building even bigger muscles would no longer enhance their performance. In fact, muscles that are too bulky can even take away from a figure skater's abilities and performance.

Large muscles are often inefficient for skaters because they weigh more than lean ones. The more a figure skater weighs, the more mass he has, and the more energy it will take for him to lift himself into a jump or to propel himself across the ice before beginning a spin or a spiral. It takes more force to move heavier objects than lighter ones, because heavier objects have greater inertia. Therefore, a heavily muscled skater will use up more energy than a lightweight skater just to move his greater mass across the ice. He may tire sooner, and he may not be able to accomplish certain feats such as triple or quadruple jumps because it will take more strength to lift his greater mass off the ice. "In terms of body composition, for maximum jumping ability and to reduce the stress of landing, skaters must stay extremely lean," says Charles Poliquin, a strength coach for Olympians and professional athletes worldwide. "Further, the technical nature of the sport means that athletes must stay lean year-round, avoiding weight fluctuations that could affect jumping ability."[31] This is because skaters do not train and practice their jumps for a single season just a few months out of the year, but all year long.

The trend toward leanness favors no one more than the female partner of a pairs skater, since the male skater must lift her overhead, carry her across the ice, and spin her into jumps at various parts of the routine. A bulky, muscular body is an advantage for the male partner of a pair but a disadvantage for the woman. Pairs skaters, especially, require carefully designed training programs to make sure they build the strength and endurance to carry out a routine but add no extra bulk to their bodies. Muscles that are too heavy could weigh them down and affect their performance. Even worse, they could result in a skating accident.

Accidents on the Ice

One figure skating accident in recent history took place during the Skate America competition in Pittsburgh, Pennsylvania, in 2004. Maxim Marinin lifted his partner, Tatiana Totmianina, off the ice and was holding her over his head

FIGURE EIGHT

Skating Firsts and Lasts

The 1960 Olympic Winter Games in Squaw Valley, California, were the last Olympics to stage figure skating events outdoors. They were also the first Olympics to be televised.

as he did a spread eagle—his legs straight and apart, his toes pointed outward as he skated in a sideways curve. Totmianina had her own legs spread out to the sides and had her arms straight down so she could clasp hands with Marinin. The lift seemed to be going as planned until Marinin's skate blades lost their grip on the ice. His legs slid out from under him and he fell forward. Totmianina plummeted several feet, landing face-first on the ice. She lay there motionless while emergency workers scrambled to her side. Totmianina suffered a concussion—when her head struck the ice, her brain ricocheted back and forth against the inside of her skull. Concussions are very serious injuries because they can cause the brain to swell and bleed. Some concussions can cause lasting brain damage, and they can even be deadly.

Fortunately for Totmianina, the concussion was not severe. She was released with a black eye and a swollen face after one night in the hospital, and she was able to resume training within a few short weeks. "In pairs skating you fall

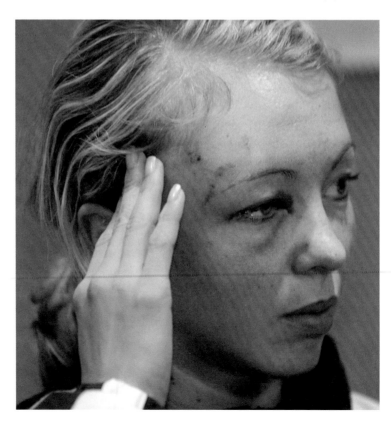

Tatiana Totmianina holds the side of her injured head at a press conference following her fall at the Skate America competition in 2004. Totmianina suffered a black eye, scrapes, and a concussion, but she was able to resume training a few weeks later.

sometimes," she told news reporters the day after the accident. "Actually, it wasn't something unusual; it was just a simple lift. It wasn't successful."[32]

A fall like Totmianina's may not be unusual among pairs skaters, but it did showcase the dangerous nature of figure skating and the kinds of injuries that can happen on the ice. Skaters strive to make their performances look magical and to appear as if they are gliding and twirling effortlessly across the rink, but skating puts tremendous strain on the skater's body. "Figure skating is one of the sports where you can get a bad injury, especially pairs skating, because there are . . . lifts and throw jumps and some other elements that are extremely dangerous," says Oleg Vasiliev, coach to Totmianina at the time of her 2004 accident. "It's high speed and very high momentum so sometimes it's very difficult to handle these movements. … Doing this kind of sport you should be ready for something like this to happen."[33]

Acute Versus Long-Term Injuries

Totmianina suffered from an acute injury—one that happens when a sudden, traumatic event like a collision or a fall causes bodily harm. Acute injuries happen often in figure skating, especially in pairs skating in which men lift or twirl or toss their partners. Since two people work together in pairs skating, either one can make a mistake that results in injury, and often the female member of the pair is the one to take the fall. Individual skaters also fall frequently, especially when learning new moves such as jumps. In fact, even experienced skaters may fall several times during every practice session. Not all of these falls result in serious acute injuries like broken bones or concussions, especially since skaters quickly learn how to fall on the ice—they take advantage of ice's slippery nature and try to fall on their side in a skidding motion, so that the impact of the fall is a glancing blow, spread out over the sliding distance as opposed to landing straight down with their full body weight hitting the ice hard all at once. Nevertheless, ice-skating is a sport where serious, acute injuries do happen.

ANKLE SPRAINS

Ankle sprains are a common acute injury among figure skaters, reportedly affecting 23 percent of skaters. A sprain happens when one or more of the five ankle ligaments are partially or completely torn. Skaters can decrease their chances of an ankle sprain by wearing properly fitting skating boots.

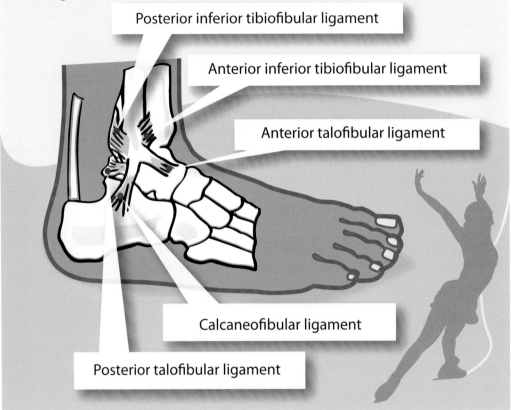

Posterior inferior tibiofibular ligament

Anterior inferior tibiofibular ligament

Anterior talofibular ligament

Calcaneofibular ligament

Posterior talofibular ligament

Source: U.S. Figure Skating www.usfsa.org/Shell.asp?sid=28765

Even more common than the occasional fall, which can result in an acute injury like a concussion or a broken bone, are chronic injuries, also called overuse injuries. These are injuries that happen over a long time period. When a certain joint or muscle is used every day over and over in the same way, such as landing a figure skating jump, each repeated movement can cause a tiny amount of damage to the body. This damage builds up over time, and eventually it can cause a skater significant pain or even disability. "Competitive figure skating has evolved into a very physically demanding sport," says kinesiologist Semyon Slobounov.

Single skaters need to incorporate more double, triple, and quadruple jumps into their routine, while pair skaters must execute more throws and lifts in order to impress judges and receive national recognition for their complex coordination skills. … This results in elite figure skaters training at least four to six hours per day, six times per week, for ten to eleven months per year. Such rigorous physical fitness demands lead to a number of acute and overuse injuries.[34]

Foot Fallouts

The leather boot of a figure skate fits tightly around the foot to support the ankle, but this design can wreak havoc on the bones of the foot. Bunions are one common malady, afflicting 57 percent of figure skaters. Bunions occur when toes are crammed into a narrow space and the big toe angles toward the others, forming a painful bony bump at the base of the big toe. Another foot problem, affecting nearly one in two skaters, is Haglund's deformity, a bony mass that develops on the back of the heel in response to a constant rubbing against the stiff inner surface of the skating boot. The growth causes a noticeable bump on the heel and can irritate the Achilles tendon, causing swelling and severe pain. About a third of skaters develop yet another foot condition—hammertoes. These occur when the toes are consistently forced to bend downward, which often happens in tight figure skates. The joints of the toes may stiffen into this position over time. All of these conditions can be very painful and in many cases they require surgery. Young feet with bones that are still growing are very susceptible to long-term problems, so young skaters may develop permanent foot damage.

The most common overuse injuries affecting figure skaters happen in the lower body, affecting the lower back, the legs, and especially the feet and the ankles. According to U.S. Figure Skating, 34 percent of figure skaters experience lower-back pain. About one-fourth of skaters have pain and problems in their hips or their knees. About one in four skaters also suffers from a sprained ankle at some point in his or her career, an injury caused by a twisting or wrenching motion that damages the ankle's ligaments—the fibrous tissues that hold bones together at a joint. Many skaters suffer damage to their feet, as well, often as a result of doing so much movement in tightly laced or poorly fitting skates. They may have numbness caused by damaged foot nerves, toes that become deformed, and a lump that forms on the back of the heel from the foot constantly slipping and grinding against the leather of the skating boot.

These chronic injuries can be very painful. They demonstrate the extreme physical toll that many hours of figure skating practice can take on the body. "Compared to the other sports, ice is the hardest landing surface and it has virtually no shock absorption," says Linda Tremain Baer, a former physical therapist at the Olympic Ice Arena in Lake Placid, New York. "Therefore, the joints in the foot, ankle, knee, hip, and back must do all the work to absorb the shock upon impact." Not only can repeatedly landing on an unforgiving surface like ice cause injury over time, Baer also points out that figure skates themselves are not designed with the athlete's long-term health in mind. "As figure skating boots are designed today they decrease the ability of the foot and ankle to bend," she says. "That means that a skater's foot and ankle are not able to absorb the shock as they should. Instead, the additional forces that are transferred to the knee, hip, and back can lead to unnecessary strain and load on these joints."[35] Slobounov agrees that the shape of the skate itself makes figure skating movements hard on feet and legs. "No other sport places the same diversity of forces on such a narrow base of support," he says.[36]

Although overuse injuries may range from crippling, such as lower-back pain, to annoying, like constant rubbing on the back of the heel, they can negatively affect a skater's performance. At best, throbbing pain might break the athlete's concentration during a critical move, causing him to receive lower scores. At worst, chronic injuries can bring about the end of a professional or competitive skating career. "Chronic injuries can play havoc with an athlete's motivation and most often are a major cause of burnout," says Slobounov.[37] Indeed, forcing oneself to continue the long and demanding hours of practice both on ice and off, in spite of pain, may be one of the most difficult challenges figure skaters face. It takes a special kind of athlete to commit wholeheartedly to the various and intense rigors of this sport.

CHAPTER 5

The Psychology of Figure Skating

All figure skaters fall down from time to time, even the best ones. They are always trying to master new skills and get better at their sport, and this means taking risks. Although all sports can be physically and emotionally demanding, figure skating may create even more psychological challenges than physical ones. Unlike most other sports, where athletes either compete side by side against their competitors or face them head-on as part of a team, figure skating is normally done alone or in pairs on the ice, with all eyes on the skater and everyone looking for flaws in his or her performance. Figure skaters are harshly judged on every aspect of their skating program—not just their technical skills in jumps, spirals, and spins, but the outfits they wear, the expression on their face, and the emotion they show in the rink. Competing in front of crowds and knowing they may be viciously criticized if they make a mistake puts figure skaters among the world's most pressured athletes. "It is always said that figure skating is the most revealing sport of all," says Peggy Fleming, 1968 Olympic gold medalist. "Not only are we usually all alone out on that ice, but we're being judged for so many very personal things: our costume, the music we chose, and how we move to that music. It's very hard to hide the kind of person you really are with so many aspects of your personality being watched."[38]

To cope with the physical demands of their sport and the intense emotional stress that goes along with the fear of making mistakes, figure skaters need to train for psychological strength and fortitude as much as for physical fitness. Every skating routine requires physical strength and stamina but also an emotional connection with the music and with the crowd. Skaters are judged harshly on the technical aspects of their programs, such as whether they completed the required type and number of jumps and spins and how well these elements were performed, but the other half of their score evaluates how well they skated to the song they chose, whether they timed their movements to the beat of the music, and whether they captured the feeling of the song in their skating. Thus, figure skaters must do far more on the ice than just complete challenging stunts. They have to be artists as well, linking the way they skate to the rhythm and feeling of the song they chose. They are performers, trying hard to win over the audience, and most importantly, the judges. The job is so difficult that it often takes a lifetime of training and practice to get right.

FIGURE EIGHT

Fan Favorite

Figure skating is the fifth most popular spectator sport in the United States. Professional football, college football, Major League Baseball, and professional basketball are the only sports that have more American fans.

Starting Young

So much must be learned in order to skate well that most figure skaters take up the sport during childhood. Many of them practically grow up on the ice. The average age for boys to begin skating is ten years old. Girls start younger still, at six years old on average. Skating programs throughout the United States and in many other countries provide lessons for these young skaters, who then progress to higher and higher levels by passing skating tests, routines they perform in front of judges. Every skating level requires harder skills, and a skater cannot move on to higher levels until he or she passes each level in order. At a very young age, most skaters become used

to the fact that they must skate before crowds and be judged on their performance. This in itself can be difficult for children, who may feel performance anxiety—emotional stress that occurs when performing for others. Anxiety can make a person sweat, feel shaky, and even get sick to her stomach. Fear of being in front of an audience, of making a mistake, or of failing the skating test can ruin a routine if a skater does not learn to handle the pressure. "Research findings suggest that performing in front of an audience … can be enjoyable," say figure skating coach Eva Monsma and kinesiologist Deborah Feltz, "but if accompanied by falling can catastrophically turn into a source of stress and anxiety." In fact, they say, the stress of a single error can ruin an entire program. "It is not unusual for skaters to have a spectacular performance until a fall with subsequent falls on even otherwise simple elements."[39] When one error follows another, even on techniques the skater has mastered, it becomes clear that the emotional stress of performing has a physical effect on figure skaters.

Young skaters who move to higher and higher skating levels do so by learning how to cope with performance anxiety. Many work with sports psychologists, professionals who help athletes deal with stress, anxiety, and other mental and emotional aspects of their sport. A sports psychologist identifies things that make an athlete anxious and suggests ways to cope with stress in healthy ways. Some athletes may practice techniques like visualization, where they picture themselves succeeding at their performance. Others may meditate before a competition, trying to clear their heads of disquieting thoughts in order to calm their nerves. Many skaters draw their routines out on paper to help them memorize the steps, then mentally move through their routines while listening to the music. For many skaters this technique calms them down and helps them prepare to step out on the ice. These are just some of the ways skaters can deal with the pressures of performing for audiences and judges.

A coach works with a young girl during a figure skating lesson. Competitive skaters typically take up the sport when they are very young and must quickly learn to cope with performance anxiety.

Golden Teen

At the 1998 Winter Olympics in Nagano, Japan, U.S. figure skating phenomenon Michelle Kwan was favored to bring home a gold medal. A seasoned skating champion with many competitions under her belt, Kwan seemed sure to win. However, she had lost the U.S. national and world figure skating championships the year before. Both titles went to another American skater, a newcomer from Texas named Tara Lipinski, just fourteen years old at the time. At the Nagano Olympics, Kwan's skating routines had a few flaws. Lipinski, age fifteen by then, was already known for pulling off difficult technical feats like a triple loop jump combination—two triple jumps performed back to back, something no other female skater had ever performed successfully. Lipinski skated a difficult program nearly flawlessly in Nagano. It was enough to beat Kwan and earn Lipinski the gold medal, making her the youngest individual gold medalist in the history of the Winter Olympics. Lipinski holds that title to this day, just edging out 1928 teen gold medalist Sonja Henie. These champions demonstrate the young age at which many figure skaters take up the sport in order to qualify for Olympic competition.

Lipinski looks at her gold medal after her thrilling win at the 1998 Olympic Games.

However skaters learn to control the stress of performing, their coping skills are something that they must rely on more and more as the years go by. The better a figure skater becomes, the more intense the competition and the more stressful the sport can be. Young figure skaters who show the potential to excel sometimes feel pressure not just from themselves, but from fellow skaters and also people they look up to. "The pressure to win can come from parents, coaches, peers, sponsors, and even the media," say kinesiologists Ron Pfeiffer and Brent Mangus. "The stress of competition may result in significant problems for some kids."[40] Figure skating can be expensive and time consuming, too, so young skaters often feel that their parents have invested a lot of time and money in their skating. If they do not live up to expectations, they may feel a terrible sense of failure. All of this makes figure skating an emotional, not just a physical, challenge for competitors, and the stress of it may continue throughout a skater's career. All figure skaters must learn to cope with stress if they are to be successful.

Gambling on Skates

The better a figure skater becomes the more chances he or she must take to succeed professionally. Once skaters reach a skating level where they start to compete against others, the judges are no longer evaluating them on whether they have passed a test and can move on to a new level but are instead deciding who gave the best performance of the day. Competitive-skating programs have required elements, such as a certain number of double or triple jumps and certain styles of spins or spirals that must be included in the program. If even one element is left out, or if the skater makes a mistake such as falling when trying to land a jump, the judges will award fewer points to that skater and he is unlikely to meet his ultimate goal—to win a medal for first, second, or third place.

Skating competitions do leave a certain number of things up to the skaters. Free-skate programs let skaters choose the elements they want to put into their routines. Skaters try to incorporate the most difficult elements they can successfully complete, because these get more points from the judges. For example, a skater may plan to include quadruple jumps in a free-skate program to get higher points, even if he fears he will not be able to complete a quadruple. His coach may even push for the more challenging jump. "Coaches frequently take chances of including nearly mastered elements to gain a competitive edge," say Monsma and Feltz, "but this practice undoubtedly heightens the stakes for competing skaters."[41]

Orser performs a jump during his free-skate routine at the 1988 Winter Olympics. A slight mistake at the beginning of his program seemingly affected his confidence as he continued his performance, and his choice to substitute a planned triple Axel with a double Axel cost him the gold medal.

Difficult free-skate programs are always a gamble. If a skater succeeds at the quadruple jumps, he may beat competitors who only did triple jumps, but if he falls during one of the jumps, he may lose to competitors who successfully completed their easier triples. Complicating the situation is the fact that skaters rarely know what their competitors are planning to do. If all the other skaters have quadruple jumps in their programs, a skater who completes only a triple jump will get fewer points for it, and he will lose unless the competitors performing quadruple jumps fall or have other errors in their programs. Often, a competitive skater completes his routine and then begins a stressful wait in the hope that other skaters will fall or make mistakes.

Such was the case in the 1988 Winter Olympics in Calgary, Alberta, Canada. Canadian champion Brian Orser and U.S. favorite Brian Boitano faced off in a skating duel that

A Famous Figure Skating Scuffle

In January 1994 America's best figure skaters were training for the Olympic trials to determine who would make the U.S. figure skating team that year. Top picks were rivals Nancy Kerrigan and Tonya Harding, both of whom were believed to have a chance at the women's Olympic gold. On January 6, a man attacked Kerrigan as she exited an ice rink after a practice session. He smashed her kneecaps with a baton, then ran off. Days later, three men were arrested in the attack. One of them, Jeff Gillooly, was accused of hiring someone to break Kerrigan's leg and thwart her Olympic hopes. The scandal intensified when it was revealed that Gillooly was Harding's ex-husband.

Kerrigan's injuries were not severe. She not only made the U.S. Olympic team, she won silver at the Olympics that February. Harding, too, made the team, but only placed eighth at the Games. She

was later tried and convicted for lying to investigators about her part in Kerrigan's attack. Harding was heavily fined and was banned from competitive figure skating for life. The ordeal did much for the sport's popularity, however. Women's figure skating was by far the most-watched Olympic event that year.

Harding, left, and Kerrigan practice prior to their performances at the 1994 Olympic Games.

became known around the world as the Battle of the Brians. Going into the free-skate program, the scores were neck and neck. Orser had received slightly higher scores in the short-skate program with the required elements that all skaters must complete. However, Boitano's scores were only slightly behind and kept him in striking range for a gold medal. Boitano skated first during the free-skate program, and he knew he had to take big risks. He performed eight triple jumps, two of them in difficult jump combinations, all of which he landed flawlessly. Despite Boitano's performance, Orser stepped onto the ice looking extremely confident. He was already ahead of Boitano. He had only to pull off a perfect free-skate program to win the gold medal.

The battle was far from over, however, and Orser's confidence wavered after he flubbed the takeoff of the first triple jump in his program and ended up landing it on two feet, something that results in a slight point deduction from judges. As so often happens under the pressure of an intense skating competition, the slight mistake seemed to affect the rest of Orser's program. Seemingly exhausted, he ended up replacing a triple Axel jump with an easier double Axel toward the end of his program. This ultimately gave Boitano the edge in the competition. By a narrow margin, Boitano won gold, with five of the nine judges favoring him and the other four favoring Orser. It was one of the most famous battles in figure skating history and showcased the intense psychological pressure that can affect these athletes. "When a skater steps on the ice to compete," Boitano says, "the nerves, tension, and sheer suspense of that moment make for great drama."[42]

Double the Pressure

When singles skaters like Boitano and Orser take to the ice, they often feel very alone. All eyes are on them, watching for the slightest flaw in their appearance or performance and ready to pounce on any errors with a deduction in scores. Pairs skaters face the crowd's scrutiny together, but this does not seem to lessen the pressures of competition. Sharing a routine on the ice often causes even more intense

stress. If one skater of the pair makes a mistake, it could cost both athletes a winning score. The skater who makes the mistake may feel terrible guilt about it. The skater who did not make the error, on the other hand, may feel resentment toward the partner who did. Pairs skating introduces a whole new element of fear and worry into a skating competition. The two must rely on each other if they are going to win, and a mistake carries double the sting because it hurts someone else's scores too.

Another cause of anxiety in pairs skating is the added risk of injury if something were to go wrong. The female partner often has to overcome fear that she will be dropped in front of spectators and that this could cause serious injury as well as humiliation. This fear may be stronger if she has been dropped before. The male partner has to overcome his own fear that he might drop his partner and seriously injure her. Pairs skaters have all the pressure of needing to perform flawlessly, with the added stress of trusting someone else to perform flawlessly as well, all while not causing or receiving an injury.

A female pairs skater falls while being spun by her partner during a routine. Pairs skaters face the added pressure of having their partners be dependent upon them in order to fare well in competition.

Growing Bodies, Changing Perceptions

The stresses of pairs skating are not limited to achieving perfection in the routine. Pairs skating is also where many girls and young women become the most aware of their bodies and develop a quest for perfection. In pairs skating, the female partner is lifted overhead, spun around in the air, and even thrown into jumps. The less she weighs, the easier it will be for her male partner to accomplish these feats. The female partner in a skating pair, therefore, may feel tremendous pressure to stay thin. Weight gain could affect her partner's ability to lift her and could even put an end to her career as a pairs skater. Fear of weight gain often becomes a major source of anxiety for the female partner of a skating duo.

Pairs skaters are not the only ones who struggle with their body image. It is something that widely affects all figure skaters, especially girls and young women. In a sport where their appearance is closely and constantly scrutinized during competition, figure skaters are intensely aware of the fact that people are watching for flaws. Since they often wear short skirts and skimpy outfits during competition, female skaters feel pressure to be slender so they look good in their costumes. Adding to the problem is the practice some coaches have of weighing skaters regularly and publicly posting their weight and their body mass index (BMI)—the relationship between one's height and weight, as a measure of how much mass is in the body.

Further complicating the situation is the fact that many figure skaters take up the sport as children, when they are naturally thin and lanky. However, once they begin to go through puberty, a period during adolescence when the young body undergoes physical changes to become a sexually mature adult, young women naturally gain weight as their bodies replace some of their muscle mass with fat. These changes are normal, healthy, and unavoidable, but sadly, young skaters may try to fight the changes of adolescence by extreme dieting. "A seemingly simple comment like 'your skating dress is getting a little tight' in the intensely competitive young athlete may cause them to experience feelings of self-doubt and fear of losing

BODY MASS INDEX (BMI)

BMI

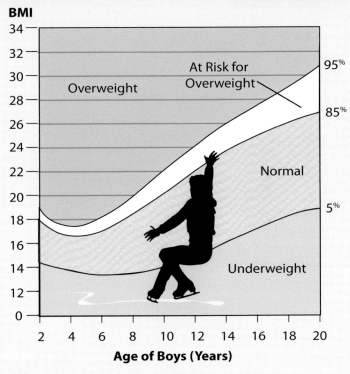

Age of Boys (Years)

To calculate your BMI:
1) Multiply your weight in pounds by 703
2) Divide the answer by your height in inches
3) Divide the answer by your height in inches again

BMI

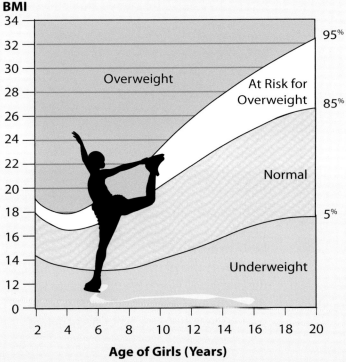

Age of Girls (Years)

Body Mass Index is a measurement taken by comparing a person's height and weight to determine whether they are within a healthy weight range. Body Mass Index does not differentiate between body fat and muscle mass, and so may not always accurately indicate whether someone is at a healthy weight. Figure skaters typically have a lower BMI than the average individual, but they may still develop insecurities or eating disorders if they feel pressured to be thinner for competition.

acceptance in their sport because they perceive their weight is outside the acceptable range," say sports medicine practitioners Sami Rifat and James Moeller.[43] All this attention to weight, appearance, and BMI has a negative effect on many figure skaters. One study found that 93 percent of female figure skaters worry about their weight, and 100 percent of those who took part in the study said they had used weight-control methods such as dieting.

Dieting Can Become a Disorder

Some figure skaters, especially girls and women, take weight control to extreme measures. They sometimes go beyond mere dieting and develop eating disorders such as anorexia nervosa, a psychological condition in which the person has an intense fear of gaining weight and begins to perceive herself as being overweight, even if she is actually very thin. People with anorexia nervosa eat very little and may even fast (avoid food altogether) if they perceive they may be gaining weight. They can quickly become undernourished, which has a negative effect on their health and their organ systems. Left untreated, anorexia nervosa can be fatal. Sufferers may actually starve themselves to death.

Bulimia nervosa is a related eating disorder. Like anorexia, it is a psychological condition in which the person believes he or she is overweight. Unlike anorexia, however, a person with bulimia develops a pattern of binge eating: Eating large amounts of food with little self-control. These binges are followed by immediately trying to get rid of the food by forced vomiting or using laxatives (medication that causes diarrhea) or diuretics (substances that cause the body to get rid of liquid). Such behavior can harm the tissues of the throat and the intestines, which become irritated by diarrhea or vomiting, and can also result in dehydration, or a lack of sufficient

FIGURE EIGHT

Medal Mania

The United States has won at least one figure skating medal at every Olympic Games since 1948—a total of seventeen consecutive Olympics.

The Threat of Being Too Thin

Eating disorders like anorexia nervosa and bulimia nervosa have a higher death toll than any other mental disorder. An estimated 4 to 5 percent of those who develop an eating disorder do not survive it—they may become so malnourished and underweight that they die of heart failure or organ failure, or they may become clinically depressed and commit suicide. Eating disorders are serious illnesses that require prompt medical intervention. Unfortunately, only about one in ten people with an eating disorder seeks treatment for it, according to the National Association of Anorexia Nervosa and Associated Disorders. Recognizing warning signs of a potential eating disorder could save a life. Red flags might include a person's being preoccupied with body image and weight, refusing food or eating only tiny portions, eating only in private, experiencing dramatic weight loss, obsessing about exercise, feeling cold all the time, growing fine hair all over the body (the body's response to feeling cold due to being underweight), and using medications such as diet pills or drugs that cause vomiting, diarrhea, or excessive urination. Getting treatment early in the illness makes recovery easier, so friends and family members should show support while encouraging the person to seek professional help.

fluids in the body. Like anorexia nervosa, the habits developed during bulimia nervosa deprive the body of nutrients it needs and can cause serious illness or death.

Unfortunately, anorexia and bulimia are common conditions among figure skaters, especially girls and women. According to the National Association of Anorexia Nervosa and Associated Disorders, 13 percent of athletes who participate in sports that are judged on grace and aesthetics (such as figure skating) develop an eating disorder. Female athletes in these sports have the highest risk. Because it is extremely important for skaters to get proper nutrition in order to hold up during long hours of practice and hard

Sarah Hughes is surrounded by media as she returns to high school following her gold-medal win at the 2002 Olympic Games. Because of the demands of their sport, skaters often struggle to balance their skating, academic, and social lives.

physical activity, eating disorders and stress about one's body image are among the most important psychological issues that figure skaters, coaches, and sports psychologists must address.

For the Love of the Sport

Stress and body image are not a figure skater's only psychological challenges. Figure skaters also face the difficulties of balancing a normal life with the pursuit of a sport that makes extreme demands on them physically, emotionally, and even socially. Because most figure skaters begin practicing the sport at a young age, those who continue on toward higher levels of competition often make sacrifices in other areas of their lives. They have to arrange time-consuming

practice schedules while also going to school, doing home-work, and perhaps having a job to help pay for their training. Many figure skaters find that most of their friends are skaters too, and they may even develop romantic relationships with other skaters because they rarely see other people outside of the sport. "Helping skaters lead a balanced life in academic, social, and sport domains can be one of the greatest challenges," say Monsma and Feltz. "Balancing skating with school or work and having a social life due to training demands are confirmed sources of stress."[44]

Even with these challenges, figure skating remains a very popular sport around the world. Despite the rigorous training schedules, the difficult routines that must be learned, the injuries that can arise from spending so much time on the ice, and the stress of performing in front of audiences and judges, figure skating remains one of the world's most popular sports to watch, and to take part in. The smiles that skaters put on their faces as they soar around the rink to music are genuine. Athletes willing to give their all on the ice do so for the love of the sport. No other athletic pastime in the world blends creativity and physical fitness, art and science, beauty and athleticism, quite like figure skating can. The human race has a long-standing love for figure skating, and it is a sport that will continue to dazzle fans for generations.

Chapter 1: A History of Figure Skating

1. Ellyn Kestnbaum. *Culture on Ice: Figure Skating and Cultural Meaning.* Middletown, CT: Wesleyan University Press, 2003, p. 57, emphasis added.
2. Kestnbaum. *Culture on Ice*, p. 59.
3. Kestnbaum. *Culture on Ice*, p. 58.
4. Irving Brokaw. *The Art of Skating: Its History and Development, with Practical Directions.* New York: Charles Scribner's Sons, 1910, p. 21.
5. Kestnbaum. *Culture on Ice*, p. 66.
6. Mary Louise Adams. *Artistic Impressions: Figure Skating, Masculinity, and the Limits of Sport.* Toronto, ON: University of Toronto Press, 2011, p. 145.
7. Adams. *Artistic Impressions*, p. 146.

Chapter 2: Physical Properties of Skates and Skating Surfaces

8. Mariana Gosnell. *Ice: The Nature, the History, and the Uses of an Astonishing Substance.* Chicago: University of Chicago Press, 2005, pp. 9–10.
9. T. Maxwell Witham, *A System of Figure Skating*, London: Horace Cox, 1897, p. 103.

10. Merrell Noden. "The Quick Chill: Will Marc Norman's Secret Ice Recipe Set Speed Skating Records in Salt Lake City?" *Popular Science*, February 2002, p. 56.
11. Vancouver 2010 International Olympic Committee. "Olympic Ice Making." Vancouver, BC, 2010, p. 1. www.eyeontheice.com/documents/ olympic ice making.pdf.
12. Carole Shulman. *The Complete Book of Figure Skating.* Champaign, IL: Human Kinetics, 2002, p. 17.
13. Shulman. *Complete Book of Figure Skating*, p. 12.
14. Shulman. *Complete Book of Figure Skating*, p. 19.

Chapter 3: The Physics of Figure Skating

15. William Charles Whiting and Stuart Rugg. *Dynatomy: Dynamic Human Anatomy.* Vol. 10. Champaign, IL: Human Kinetics, 2006, p. 110.
16. Whiting and Rugg. *Dynatomy*, p. 109.
17. Nancy Kerrigan and Mary Spencer. *Artistry on Ice: Figure Skating Skills and Style.* Champaign, IL: Human Kinetics, 2003, p. 5.
18. Whiting and Rugg. *Dynatomy*, p. 99.

19. Whiting and Rugg. *Dynatomy*, p. 99.
20. Kerrigan and Spencer. *Artistry on Ice*, p. 6.
21. Steve Miller. *The Complete Idiot's Guide to the Science of Everything.* New York: Penguin, 2008, p. 36.
22. John Eric Goff. *Gold Medal Physics: The Science of Sports.* Baltimore: Johns Hopkins University Press, 2010, p. 98.
23. Quoted in Beverly Smith. *Figure Skating: A Celebration.* Toronto, ON: McClelland & Stewart, 1999, p. xi.
24. Quoted in Juliet Macur. "Tricky at Every Turn, the Quad Can Make or Break a Routine." *New York Times,* January 13, 2010. www.nytimes.com/2010/01/14/sports/olympics/14skate.html?pagewanted=all.
25. Kerrigan and Spencer. *Artistry on Ice*, p. 129.
26. Kerrigan and Spencer. *Artistry on Ice*, p. 129.

Chapter 4: Fitness and Injuries in Figure Skating

27. Shulman. *Complete Book of Figure Skating*, p. 24.
28. J. M. Moran. "Figure Skating." In *Women in Sports* Vol. 8 of *Encyclopedia of Sports Medicine*, edited by Barbara L. Drinkwater. Malden, MA: Blackwell Science, 2010, p. 524.
29. Ron C. Judd. *The Winter Olympics: An Insider's Guide to the Legends, the Lore, and Events of the Games.,* Seattle: Mountaineers, 2009, p. 97.
30. Shulman. *Complete Book of Figure Skating*, p. 31.
31. Charles Poliquin. "The Athlete's Training Diary: A Classic Workout for Figure Skating." www.charlespoliquin.com/ArticlesMultimedia/Articles/Article/260/The_Athletes_Training_Diary_A_Classic_Workout_for_.aspx.
32. Quoted in "Tatiana Totmianina Released from Mercy Hospital." U.S. Figure Skating. October 24, 2004. www.usfsa.org/event_story.asp?id=27535.
33. Quoted in "Tatiana Totmianina Released from Mercy Hospital."
34. Semyon M. Slobounov. *Injuries in Athletics: Causes and Consequences.* New York: Springer, 2008, p. 219.
35. Linda Tremain. "Boot Problems and Boot Solutions." U.S. Figure Skating. July 2004. www.usfsa.org/content/Boot%20Problems%20and%20Boot%20Solutions.pdf.
36. Slobounov. *Injuries in Athletics*, p. 220.
37. Slobounov. *Injuries in Athletics*, p. 4.

Chapter 5: The Psychology of Figure Skating

38. Quoted in Brian Boitano. *Boitano's Edge: Inside the Real World of Figure Skating.* New York: Simon & Schuster, 1997, p. 7.
39. Eva A. Monsma and Deborah L. Feltz. "A Mental Preparation Guide for Figure Skaters." In *The Sport Psychologist's Handbook: A Guide for Sport-Specific Performance,*

edited by Joaquín Dosil. Chichester, England: John Wiley & Sons, 2006, p. 435.

40. Ronald P. Pfeiffer and Brent C. Mangus. *Concepts of Athletic Training*, 6th ed. Sudbury, MA: Jones & Bartlett Learning, 2011, p. 58.

41. Monsma and Feltz. "Mental Preparation Guide," pp. 431–432.

42. Brian Boitano. *Boitano's Edge: Inside the Real World of Figure Skating.* New York: Simon & Schuster, 1997, p. 9.

43. Sami F. Rifat and James L. Moeller. "Figure Skating." In *Bull's Handbook of Sports Injuries*, 2nd ed., edited by William O. Roberts. Columbus, OH: McGraw-Hill, 2004, p. 565.

44. Monsma and Feltz. "Mental Preparation Guide," p. 458.

GLOSSARY

angular (rotational) momentum: The momentum, or force of movement, of a rotating object.

axis of rotation: The center point or line around which a rotating object spins.

body mass index: The ratio of a person's height to his or her weight.

center of gravity: The point at which the total mass of an object or body is exactly centered.

friction: A force of resistance created when one object moves across another.

gravity: The force of attraction between all objects that have mass.

humidity: The amount of water vapor present in the air.

inertia: The tendency of a moving object to remain in motion or a still object to remain at rest unless acted upon by an outside force.

linear momentum: The momentum, or force of movement, of an object moving in a straight or a curving line.

mass: A measure of how much matter is contained in an object.

matter: Anything that has physical substance and occupies space.

molecule: Two or more atoms bonded together to make the smallest possible unit of a chemical compound.

moment of inertia: A measurement of a spinning object's resistance to a change in its spinning motion.

momentum: A measure of the force of an object's movement, found by multiplying its mass by its velocity.

physics: The branch of science that studies matter, energy, and the interactions between the two.

radius: A straight line from the center point of a circle to its rim or edge; the measurement of this line is a circle's radius.

radius of hollow (ROH): The depth of the groove carved into the base of a skating blade.

torque: A twisting force applied to a body or object.

velocity: The speed with which an object is moving or changing position.

FOR MORE INFORMATION

Books

Joan Freese. *Play-by-Play Figure Skating*. Minneapolis: Lerner, 2004. Freese discusses the history, rules, and techniques of figure skating, with instructions and photographs explaining how to carry out the different moves.

James R. Hines. *Figure Skating: A History*. Champaign: University of Illinois Press, 2006. This book begins with mythological tales about skating from its earliest days, then discusses the technical and cultural advances that have carried the sport into the modern era. It includes hundreds of photographs and profiles of famous skaters.

Rikki Samuels. *Kid's Book of Figure Skating*. New York: Citadel, 2004. Written by a gold-medal skater, this book explains how new skaters can get started, with sections for beginning, intermediate, and advanced skaters as well as for fans of the sport.

Periodicals

Pam Belluck. "Science Takes to the Ice." *New York Times,* June 22, 2009. www .nytimes.com/2009/06/23/science/ 23skate.html?pagewanted=all.

Discusses new technology designed to analyze and prevent injuries common to today's figure skaters.

Kenneth Chang. "Explaining Ice: The Answers Are Slippery." *New York Times*, February 21, 2006. www .nytimes.com/2006/02/21/science/ 21ice.html?pagewanted=all. Addresses misunderstandings about the physical makeup of ice and explains what makes it slick enough to skate on.

Clara Moskowitz. "The Physics of Figure Skating," LiveScience.com. www.livescience.com/6120-physics -figure-skating.html. Explains the physics concepts of inertia, momentum, and friction and how they apply to figure skating.

Websites

IceNetwork.com (http://web.icenetwork.com/about/index.jsp). This subsidiary of U.S. Figure Skating delivers year-round updates on figure skating stars and news worldwide, while offering fans an opportunity to interact with favorite athletes.

International Figure Skating Magazine (www.ifsmagazine.com/sections/ articles/articles). This site links to current magazine content and is regularly updated with new articles about the sport, stars, and practice of figure skating.

The Science of Jumping and Rotating (http://btc.montana.edu/olympics/physbio/biomechanics/bio-intro.html). This site, developed by the Department of Physics and Biomechanics at Montana State University, explains in detail the physics and biomechanics behind common skating maneuvers, with interactive activities and videos to help readers understand important science concepts.

U.S. Figure Skating (www.usfsa.org). The website of the official figure skating regulatory organization offers information on figure skating history, current and previous U.S. skaters and champions, skating rules and judging criteria, and how new skaters can get involved with the sport.

INDEX

W

Waltz jumps, 54
Weight training, 63–64
Whiting, William Charles, 42–43,
    47–48
Witham, T. Maxwell, 28
Women, 86, 88

Women's competitive skating, 20–22
World Figure Skating Championships,
    18, 20

Z

Zamboni, Frank, 26
Zamboni machine, 26, *26*

PICTURE CREDITS

Cover: © Valeriy Lebedev/ShutterStock.com; © Mike Powello/Allsport Concepts/Getty Images; © Robert Decelis LTD/The Image Bank/Getty Images

© AP Images/Craig Lassig, 31

© AP Images/Darron Cummings, 66

© AP Images/Doug Mills, 83

© AP Images/Keith Srakocic, 70

© AP Images/Marcio Sanchez, 64

© AP Images/Rick Bowmer, 85

© Barry Chin/The Boston Globe via Getty Images, 67

© Corbis Bridge/Alamy, 78

© Dennis Clark/Getty Images, 90

© Eileen Langsley/Figure Skating/Alamy, 39

Gale, Cengage Learning, 22, 36, 50, 72, 87

© Gilbert Iuntd; Jean-Yves Ruszniewski/TempSport/Corbis, 82

© ID1974/ShutterStock.com, 29, 42, 44

Illustrated London News/Hulton Archive/Getty Images, 15

© Jean-Yves Ruszniewski/TempSport/Corbis, 53

© Jerome Prevost/TempSport/Corbis, 63

© Kenneth Eward/Photo Researchers, Inc., 25

© Matthew Stockman/Getty Images, 48

© North Wind Picture Archives/Alamy, 17

© Olga Besnard/ShutterStock.com, 47, 51

© PCN Photography/Alamy, 26

© Shaun Botterill/Allsport/Getty Images, 80

© STF/AFP/Getty Images, 37

© testing/ShutterStock.com, 57, 68

© The Art Archive/Amoret Tanner Collection/The Picture Desk, Inc., 12

© The Art Archive/Museum of London/The Picture Desk, Inc., 9

© Underwood & Underwood/Corbis, 19

Universal Images Group via Getty Images, 60

© Yasonya/ShutterStock.com, 34

Jenny MacKay is the author of numerous nonfiction books for middle-grade and teen readers. She lives with her husband, son, and daughter in northern Nevada, about an hour's drive from Squaw Valley, site of the 1960 Winter Olympics. She is a dedicated fan of both the Summer Olympic and the Winter Olympics, and figure skating is her favorite winter event.